MY OBSESSION
WITH THE BEATLES

Amit Kshirsagar

The photo on the cover was taken by the author, when he visited Liverpool.

ISBN-10: 1494432161
ISBN-13: 9781494432164

CONTENTS

PREFACE

I was fascinated by The Beatles and their music from the age of five. As soon as I returned from kindergarten each day, I watched the popular Hal Bradox cartoon series, which depicted The Beatles, and danced merrily to their beat with my toy guitar in hand. My parents are first-generation Asian Indian immigrants to the United States of America, but I was born in America. My parents did not know anything about The Beatles. Elvis Presley was the movie super star they knew most about. They wondered who these Beatles were, as they watched my fascination grow. Very few first generation Indian immigrants knew about The Beatles. Instead, they enjoyed Indian Classical and Cine-music from their newly purchased cassette recorders and transistors. My Indian classmates also did not, at that time, know much about The Beatles, though they learned fast later from their American friends. Even then, they were more into Rap, Hip-Hop, and Heavy Metal. (Bobby Brown, MC Hammer, Milli Vanilli and Run DMC, were their passions).

As I grew older, I read a lot about The Beatles, listened to all of their albums, attended several concerts, and whenever there was any news item about The Beatles, I preserved those clippings. My parents and my colleagues and peers knew of my obsession and I shared lots of incidents, events and information with them, whether they wanted to hear it or not.

All this led me to believe that It was my sacred duty to make second generation immigrants – not just Indians, but all, Chinese, Koreans, Vietnamese, etc., - knowledgeable about The Beatles and how great they were. Hence, this book.

The Beatles are for the most part a cultural phenomenon of the 1960's. They have a worldwide following and unprecedented popularity. They earned it through their talent, hard work, determination, catchy harmonies and rhythm guitar beats. Their charisma, their looks, their different haircuts, their witty natures, and their charming personalities were a treasure in the music world. Their "Invasion of America" in 1964 and their subsequent performance on The Ed Sullivan Show was an epoch-making event. If all this information is not brought to the attention of the first and second generation immigrants, they will be missing a very exciting and interesting part of the history of Rock'n'Roll music.

The literature on The Beatles is vast, and no new book can add anything that is not already in print. But these books are mostly voluminous and either too detailed or about the technical aspects of their albums. The book *Way Beyond Compare* by John C. Winn is a required reading for Beatles fans and collectors, the first volume of a unique work. It goes over in detail all known and available Beatles recordings.

Winn spent 20 years sifting through, scrutinizing, organizing, and analyzing hundreds of hours of audio and video recordings – and putting them into a cohesive form. *Way Beyond Compare* has a companion volume book,

That Magic Feeling: The Beatles' Recorded Legacy, Volume Two, 1966-1970.

Other authoritative books on the Beatles by Mark Lewisohn are **The Beatles Recording Sessions**, **The Complete Beatles Chronicle**, and **The Beatles' London.**

This book is targeted specifically to those who still do not know about The Beatles. It may be called a Guide to The Beatles, or you may even call it The Beatles 101: A Primer for Newcomers.

The Beatles have occupied a substantial part of my life. In fact, whenever I feel lonely, the Beatles are a great solace to me. From my collection of their albums, I pick one at random and as I listen to it, I feel better.. I once wrote to Yoko Ono requesting her autograph, after explaining how John Lennon's death had affected me. She was gracious enough to oblige. At that time, I was going through a very difficult and hard period in my life and her autographed card helped lift my spirits.

A photograph of George Harrison, sent to me by his publicist, is another treasure of mine. My obsession with The Beatles is now so well known to my friends and relatives, that whenever they see any new item in the shops, they make it a point to present it to me. Sometimes, therefore, I get duplicates, but rather than disappoint them, I don't tell them that I already have the item. I could easily sell or return the extra item, but my love for The Beatles does not allow me to do so. The day George Harrison died, I received many condolence messages. My friends and parents were concerned as to how I would be able to bear the grief.

Whether still living or gone, The Beatles' music will let them live on forever in our lives.

THE BEATLES –
A FASCINATING STORY

The Rock and Roll music group known as The Beatles began in Liverpool, England in 1960. In a short span of four years, the group rose to worldwide prominence. Even after 50 years, they have still maintained their attraction. How they did this is simply mind-boggling.

All four of The Beatles came from Liverpool. The Liverpool docks were well-known to the English people for providing jobs to all, whether they were Irish, Scots, or Welch. However, by 1942, during the Second World War, Liverpool had started declining. When the Second World War ended, the Liverpool teenagers were attracted to Elvis Presley's Rock and Roll Music. John and Paul were no exception to this. They, too, were hit by the Elvis wave. John and Paul were school friends and used to hang around in the Jacaranda Coffee Bar in Liverpool. John Lennon founded a school boy band and The Beatles were born out of that.

July 6, 1957 is regarded as the date of birth of what we know today as The Beatles. John Lennon formed the Skiffle Group called The Quarry men. Paul McCartney became a friend of John, due to his guitar playing. John asked Paul to join the band, and the Beatles' era began. George Harrison joined them in 1958. At that time, Pete Best was their drummer and Brian Epstein was helping them as manager. The Quarry men became Long John and the Silver Beetles, and later, on May 10, 1960, they became The Beatles.

John Lennon humorously explained the origin of the name. "It came in a vision. A man appeared on a Flaming Pie and directed us to call ourselves The Beatles with an 'a'."

In fact, Roysten Ellis, a British poet, was the man on the Flaming Pie. Roysten invited the group for dinner and when he tried to heat up a chicken pie, it caught fire in the oven. At the time the group was the Beetles, but Roysten suggested they switch the spelling to Beatles because the group was playing Beat music and their lifestyle was the Beat way. This bit of history inspired Sir Paul McCartney, later, to call his 1997 hit album and song, *Flaming Pie*.

In 1962, Pete Best was replaced by Ringo Starr as their drummer. Before that, Ringo was in the group Rory Storm and the Hurricanes. That's where John Lennon and Brian Epstein spotted him. The addition of Ringo Starr completed the group and the course of pop music entered a new phase.

The Beatles were called a four-headed monster, because of their funny haircuts. John Lennon was the obvious leader of this group and Paul McCartney achieved the same status as John. Paul treated George Harrison as his employee in the beginning and Ringo, the drummer, was considered the least important Beatle.

Much of the credit for the huge success of The Beatles is due to their manager, Brian Epstein. He had superlative skills with which he controlled these four individuals of different attitudes and temperaments. They were efficiently managed by Epstein, until his death in 1967. Pop music history owes a lot to Brian, and no praise is enough for his contribution.

Throughout the '60s, John Lennon, Paul McCartney, George Harrison and Ringo Starr led their generation (and younger ones) into new looks, colors and modes of expression. But nothing to follow would be as sensational as the first blush of Beatlemania, when girls went crazy for these four rock idols and boys rushed to their local barbershops (in London) to get their longer locks trimmed just so.

The Beatles' power was recognized by a local talent scout, Bill Harry, who was the editor of the magazine *Mersey Beat*. He persuaded Brian Epstein to send the boys to Hamburg and open for local singing sensation, Tony Sheridan, and in August of 1960, they did just that. Tony used to imitate Elvis Presley, and Brian thought that The Beatles should also try to emulate Elvis in singing their Rock'n'Roll standards, which were known to the local German public. The crowd would shout "Mach shau, mach shau" in German, which meant "Make show, make show," and all the female audience members would rush to the front of the stage to catch a glimpse of Tony swiveling his hips like Elvis.

George Harrison was deported from Hamburg, as he was only 17 - too young to work in a nightclub after midnight. The Beatles returned to Hamburg twice in 1961-1962.

The Beatles recorded together for the first time on October 15th, 1962. George Martin, a noted Record Producer in Liverpool, offered them a contract and their first formal recording session was held at Abbey Road Studios. The Beatles became #1 in a popularity poll of the Liverpool music newspaper *Mersey Beat*. They also made their radio debut in 1962 in Manchester. Their first singles, *Love Me Do* and *P.S. I Love You*, were released in 1962, and their second single, *Please Please Me*, came out in 1963. It topped in both *New Musical Express* and *Disc* magazines, and they received their first Silver Disc for selling 250,000 copies.

The Beatles were about many things and changed many things. They were about music, youth, volume, energy, a post-war changing of the guard. Overnight, they redefined the way kids were supposed to look and feel. In 1963, The Beatles were seen primping before a November 1963 concert at the Coventry Theater near London. Paris was disquieted by this loud volley from London; France had always dictated to the British (and indeed to the wider world) when it came to food, wine and fashion. But now, increasingly, The Beatles were calling the tune.

In 1963, The Beatles appeared on Sir Lew Grade's ATV show at the London Palladium, and two days later, they appeared on the Royal Variety show attended by Queen Elizabeth, the Queen Mother, and Princess Margaret.

At a time when Americans were in a deep shock in the aftermath of President Kennedy's assassination, the Beatles energized the country and brought hope to young Americans.

Paul McCartney and John Lennon told Brian Epstein that they did not want to go to America, unless they had a #1 song. *I Want to Hold Your Hand* reached #1 in the U.S., on February 1st, 1964 and The Beatles' Revolution was under way. Walter Cronkite, the famous television journalist, was the first to interview The Beatles when they came to America. Cronkite hoped to attract young people to watch the CBS Evening News.

Their next stop was a performance on The Ed Sullivan Show which was viewed by 73 million people, and created such commotion and chaos that it became a sensational moment in television history. The sophistication and innovativeness of their music and lyrics held the key to the sustained success of The Beatles. Their music was innovative and had a unique style, creating a pop music revolution and mesmerizing the World.

Another highlight of the year 1964 was the production of their first film, *A Hard Day's Night*. The idea of making this movie belonged to Noel Rodgers and Paul Owenstein (both of United Artists). In this film, Paul's grandfather (played by the veteran actor Wilford Brambell) was most prominent, and The Beatles were dismissed with only a few lines. The Beatles did not like this, but decided not to complain. The main attraction of the film turned out to be their music. Capitol had not thought in 1963 that Beatles' records were suitable for the American market. So, they devised a scam. They asked The Beatles to go for a three-picture contract, giving them three soundtrack albums. *A Hard Day's Night* was the first picture of this scheme. It became so successful that U.A. made more than half a million dollars.

That was the year The Beatles began to conquer the World. Their single, *I Want To Hold Your Hand* shot to #1 on the American Billboard singles chart. Huge crowds of semi-delirious young people greeted the "Fabulous Four" in the Netherlands, Denmark, Hong Kong, Australia, and New Zealand. Beatlemania continued, making 1965 as successful as 1964. The Beatles toured in France, Italy, Spain, and America once again and finally in their native

Great Britain, where they were awarded the honorary M.B.E. (Member of the Order of the British Empire).

Books and newspapers in the last several decades have described in great detail the delirious behavior by fans when The Beatles performed on The Ed Sullivan Show in 1964, but even though the same frenzy occurred elsewhere on their U.S. tours, it was not covered so extensively by the press. For example, when The Beatles performed in Chicago, for the first time in September, 1964, their fans provided a thrill they never forgot. A crowd of 5,000 greeted them at the airport and 13,000 teenage, mostly female, concert goers showered jelly beans on their heroes. Why? Because George Harrison had innocently remarked, "Jelly beans are our favorite snack food."

There was a plan for a civic reception, for The Beatles. 100,000 people were expected to attend, but the event attracted so much attention it had to be cancelled, as there were insufficient police officers for the Fab Four.

During their debut performance in Chicago, the audience was hysterical. Not only teenagers, but even adults were uncontrollable. The police had to work hard to protect The Beatles. In answer to a question by a reporter, Ringo Starr said that the fans would have killed them, if the protection had not been there. There were 300 policemen, 150 firemen, and 200 ushers.

The show was to begin at 8:30 p.m., but fans started lining up at dawn.

The Beatles answered questions humorously. John Lennon explained that it took him longer to dry his hair because it was longer. Paul McCartney said he was looking forward to meeting Chicago's gangsters with their broad brimmed hats and wide ties.

A man in the crowd said that he had seen The Beatles in Milwaukee earlier, and that he had even touched them. The girls in the crowd wanted to touch him, because he had touched The Beatles. The man had to turn on his heels and run, because 100 girls were chasing him.

There is no way to measure, and no way to quantify Beatlemania. The intensity and pressure were off the charts. Film director Richard Lester did the best possible job of capturing the craziness in the film *A Hard Day's Night*, which portrayed a couple of days in the lives of those in the group. The credit for choosing the title, *A Hard Day's Night* goes to Ringo Starr who twisted his original expression "a hard night's work" into "*A Hard Day's Night*". This movie was about The Beatles' public image. The songs were mostly John Lennon's, but they were credited as Lennon's and McCartney's.

John Lennon was very unpredictable. When Richard Lester produced A Hard Day's Night, he often had to tell John to behave, as otherwise the whole show would be ruined. John Lennon was notorious for pushing people's buttons and creating problems. His dry sense of humor and his provocative remarks often created a backlash. However, it should also be remembered that he was kind-hearted and compassionate.

British photographer Terence Spencer, who was right there, front and center witnessing the uproar over the Beatles told LIFE's editors in New York City what was going on, not only throughout Europe, but also right outside LIFE magazine's New York offices looked like a blessing from the outside, but from the inside, it often seemed a curse. But it is undeniable, all these years later that it was nothing short of fantastic.

In the beginning, The Beatles were inexperienced and had to rely on their manager, Brian Epstein, for his guidance. However, gradually, they began to take control themselves.

<u>What Mick Jagger of The Rolling Stones had to say about The Beatles</u>

"We were doin' Chuck Berry songs and blues and things, and we thought that we were totally unique animals. And then we heard there was a group from Liverpool, and they had long hair, scruffy clothes. But they had a record contract. And they had a record on the charts, with a bluesy harmonica on it, called Love Me Do. When I heard the combination of all these things, I was almost sick... We were playing a little club in Richmond and suddenly there they were right in front of me – the Fab Four. John, Paul, George, and Ringo. The four-headed monster. They never went anywhere alone at this point. And they had on these beautiful, long black leather trench coats. I could really die for one of those. And I thought, 'Even if I have to learn to write songs, I'm gonna get this.' We went through some pretty strange times. We had a lot of rivalry in those early years and a little bit of friction. But we always ended up friends, and I'd like to think we still are. 'Cause they were some of the greatest times of our lives."

The music of The Beatles was influenced both by the guitars they used and the cars that they drove around in. In 1964, John Lennon introduced George Harrison to Rickenbacker guitar Company owner, Francis C. Hall. When Hall found out that The Beatles would be appearing on *"The Ed Sullivan Show"* in February of 1964, he rushed over to George Harrison's side, since he had tonsillitis, and was sick in bed, and showed him the Rickenbacker 360/12, which became his trademark during The Beatles' touring years (1964-1966).

The Beatles were fortunate enough to live out their fantasies of driving and riding in the cars of their dreams, whether it was John Lennon in his 1965 Rolls-Royces-Phantom V Saloons, as well as a Valentines Black model, or George Harrison's 1964 Jaguar XKE or his platinum-silver Aston Martin D B5, Paul McCartney's Goodwood Green 1966 Aston Martin D B6, and his 1967 Classic Lamborghini 400 GT 2+2, OR Ringo Starr's Facel Vega "Facel II", his 1960 190 SL, 1984 190 E or his 2000 CL 55 AMG. Of course, everyone remembers *Drive My Car* from *Rubber Soul*, but The Beatles mostly abstained from writing about cars, during their tenure as a band. Most of their notable songs about cars came only as solo-artists. This included: George Harrison's *Faster*, Ringo Starr's *In My Car*, and also Paul McCartney's *The Back Seat of My Car*.

Up to 1965, The Beatles' fans were young boys and girls, who were obsessed with the music and look of The Beatles. They used to scream and shout, rather than listen to their music. However, around 1965, and when their album *Rubber Soul* was released, more mature listeners, who understood and recognized the inherent qualities in The Beatles' music, began to become more interested in the songwriting, instrumentation and record making of The Beatles. Many adults began to admire The Beatles for their charm, musical skills and wit. The Beatles became the top grossing group in the world as they performed more on "The Ed Sullivan Show", before sell-out crowds, and completed a 26 city tour of the United States. The Beatles very much wanted to meet their hero, Elvis Presley, but Elvis was not eager to meet them. Finally, on August 27th, 1965, they got their chance; the boys had deprived Elvis of his throne and Elvis was sore about that. So the meeting did not go over very well. John Lennon therefore remarked, upon returning to England, "Where is the Elvis that we wanted to see?"

Elvis' hit song, *Hound Dog*, was written by the famous rhythm and blues-loving teenagers Jerry Leiber and Mike Stoller. They became the "King's" favorite song writers, but as the nature of the industry changed in the mid-'60s, Leiber and Stoller were not able to adapt to the new musical climate that was created by the Fab Four and Beatlemania. Even so, they felt the enormous charm of The Beatles. The Beatles submitted a demo to British Decca, which contained two of Leiber and Stoller's songs, *Searchin'*, and *Three Cool Cats*. Later, Paul recorded *Kansas City*, John did *Stand By Me* and *Hound Dog* and Ringo recorded, *I Keep Forgettin'*.

By 1965, for the public, The Beatles were like Gods. The Beatles had therefore to do something to rise to their expectation. For this, they produced their second film, *HELP*, which was in color. It was originally called *Eight Arms to Hold You*. While shooting the film *HELP* and recording the album, John and Paul were not seeing eye-to-eye. John Lennon became more withdrawn. Paul McCartney, on the contrary, was showing more energy and was producing higher quality songs. John became envious. A once brilliant John Lennon had, by this time, become just one of the four Beatles. He resented this and wrote the song, *I'm a Loser*.

In 1965, The Beatles performed in Piedmont Park Stadium in Atlanta, Georgia. More than 34,000 people attended this show. As usual, the audience was screaming. In Atlanta, the sound system was excellent, so much so that it was the only stadium where The Beatles could hear themselves over the shrieks of the fans. The Beatles' manager requested Baker Audio's Duke Mewborn, who was architect of the excellent sound system, to go with The Beatles for the rest of their shows. He declined because he did not see any future in the four guys with long hair.

The huge success of The Beatles became a problem for John Lennon. His ascendancy over Paul McCartney was over. Paul was gaining the same status as John. His song, *Eleanor Rigby* was more remarkable than Lennon's *Tomorrow Never Knows*. Paul was successfully experimenting in instrumentation, sound, language, verse, and utilizing production value and recording techniques. John was becoming more lethargic and Paul, more energetic. His song, *Got To Get You Into My Life* on the album *Revolver* rose to #8 and stayed in the Top 30 for eight weeks. However, it is to Paul's credit that he never attempted to side track John.

On the contrary, he tried hard to revive and retain their old friendship, but the decline of The Beatles had started.

Bob Eubanks, the moderator of *The Newlywed games*, was trying to arrange a Beatles concert in L.A., in 1964, when The Beatles were just starting to become stars. He had a hard time raising the money for such an endeavor. The Beatles wanted a premier venue like the Hollywood Bowl, which had 18,000 seats. Eubanks has written a very humorous account in his autobiography of all his efforts and problems surrounding The Beatles visit to L.A. He had headaches, hard work, near disasters and costly mistakes. Getting The Beatles away from the crowd was a difficult task and the tricks and decoys that were used have been described well by Eubanks. Eubanks' success with this L.A. visit of The Beatles was a first step in his TV career later.

Eubanks arranged a second concert of The Beatles in 1966. The Beatles, according to Bob, were becoming difficult and less affable. The show went well, it was a hit, but as usual, the crowd was screaming so loudly, no one could hear the band playing and the high priced sound system rented by Eubanks was useless; only the screams were amplified. It was an ordeal to get The Beatles out of the stadium safely. Due to so many items of expenditures, each Beatle received only 4,000 dollars, but Bob got more. It was, he says, his best moment, because he actually made more than The Beatles!

The Beatles' performance in 1966, at Dodger Stadium in Los Angeles, California provided the stage for the unfortunate controversy created by John Lennon's statement, "The Beatles are now more popular than Jesus Christ." This caused a furor throughout the U.S. The Beatles' manager, Brian Epstein, gave a sincere apology and clarification, but to no avail. Beatles' records were burned. They were boycotted. Their concerts lost high audience numbers, and they even received death threats.

John Lennon said, "If I had said that Rock and Roll was bigger than Jesus, I might have gotten away with it, but as it stands, I said The Beatles were bigger than Jesus, and it was taken wrong."

All of this controversy arose out of *London Daily Mirror* reporter Maureen Cleave's misquoting John. John really meant to say, "We mean more to kids than Jesus Christ, as Christianity is vanishing and shrinking."

Prior to 1966, the Lennon/McCartney songwriting partnership was unstoppable. They were recognized as the greatest songwriting duo in the twentieth century by Billboard magazine. Every album that they recorded went to #1 and Platinum. However, after the "Beatles are bigger than Jesus" remark, all this changed. Many people believe that it was Yoko Ono who broke up The Beatles, but this was not so. John Lennon had clearly suffered a major setback, from which he never fully recovered.

August 29th, 1966, was the date of their last official concert performance as a band. This was at San Francisco's famous Candlestick Park. The Beatles decided not to tour any more in 1966.

Around this time, when The Beatles were working on their album *Sgt. Pepper's Lonely Hearts Club Band*, John Lennon was not in full form, and Paul McCartney had to take the lead. This album was meant to extend the frontiers of pop recording. It was a collaborative effort, and George Martin, the producer who had recorded their first record and whose musical expertise often filled the gaps between The Beatles' raw talent and the sound they wanted to achieve, was also helping them in composing sound-effects, recording, and instrumentation. George Martin's influence was so great that some journalists called him the fifth-Beatle.

Sgt. Pepper's Lonely Hearts Club Band depicts fantastic ideas and beliefs. It conveys the temperament of the common man. The music world thought that the new Beatles were reborn, replacing the old ones. The release of this album electrified the whole world and glorified The Beatles. Not only was the idea for the name of this album Paul's, but the skill in composing all kinds of different tunes, "in a seamless whole" (as it was described by American author, Albert Goldman), bears the stamp of Paul McCartney. Paul was a perfectionist, and he made even John Lennon do repeated takes. John did not like this, and his songs did not have the same quality as Paul's, so he put the blame on Paul for destroying his songs. However, it was John Lennon's fault, because he did not know what he wanted.

The noted Beatles scholar, musicologist and contributing writer for the *Ann Arbor Observer*, Jim Leonard, has said, "The Beatles' *Sgt. Pepper's Lonely Hearts Club Band*, when it was released in 1967, was dubbed as the BEST CONCEPT ALBUM of all-time. All of the songs flowed effortlessly together into a cohesive whole, with the final climactic tremor of The Beatles timeless classic, *A Day in the Life*, bringing the entire psychedelic experience of the album to a glorious reverberation. The coda (ending) from this song has a marvelous quality of resonating in the ears of the listeners well after the ridges on the record album played by listeners of the day are complete."

The *Sgt Pepper's Lonely Hearts Club Band* album begins on a high note with all the members of the band playing in concise unity. This flows into Ringo Starr's elegant *With A Little Help from My Friends*, which is credited to Ringo Starr's alias, Billy Shears, the only name on the album. No other names are directly mentioned. The audience is left to wonder who the other members of Sgt. Pepper's Lonely Hearts Club Band are. We are once again reminded that it is The Beatles themselves! Some other memorable moments on this album are *Being for The Benefit of Mr. Kite*, which was taken directly from a poster ad for a London circus by John Lennon, and Paul McCartney's moving song *When I'm Sixty Four*, which The Beatles had written and performed during their days at the Cavern club.

In an exclusive interview on NBC's TODAY show in 1982, Paul McCartney told Bryant Gumbel how the name *Sgt. Pepper* originated. "We got the idea for the album from salt and pepper shakers," he said, "We could have called ourselves Salt and Pepper, though it didn't make sense at the time. Now it would. But, since we were no longer touring, we needed a name to give ourselves an alter-ego.

So we decided to name ourselves 'Sgt. Pepper's Lonely Hearts Club Band'. It then stuck and the rest is history."

Indeed it did stick, as one of the greatest pop LPs of all time, in the history of popular music, in the vaults of time. In 1967, the album *Sgt. Pepper's Lonely Hearts Club Band* was compared with the Beach Boys' *Pet Sounds*, for its richness in texture and fluidity in feel.

The packaging of this album was reported to cost about 1500 British pounds. When Brian Epstein asked Sir Joseph Lockwood, the head of EMI (Electronic Music Industry) for this amount, he remarked, "This is more than the cost of hiring the entire London Symphony Orchestra." Only when The Beatles promised to repay the 1500 pounds, if the album did not sell 100,000 copies, did Sir Joseph agree to bear the cost. However, the album sold 545,000,000,000 copies and The Beatles could have repaid the 1500 pounds several hundred times over. It became the album of the year in 1967 and 1968. By 2003, this album had gone Triple Platinum eight times over by The British Phonographic Industry.

The Beatles manager, Brian Epstein, died in August 1967, one month before *Sgt. Pepper's Lonely Hearts Club Band* was released. The Beatles stopped touring.

John Lennon did not like the idea of venturing out on their own. It was Brian Epstein who had always held the band together. Now, for the first time, he was gone, and the "Fab Four" were on their own completely. This was both scary and exciting for John and Paul. George began to collaborate independently with Sitar Maestro Ravi Shankar and Ringo pursued his solo acting endeavors.

The great success that The Beatles achieved from *Sgt Pepper* soon began to evaporate, because The Beatles started to have differences.

After 1967, John Lennon was becoming more and more infatuated with Avant-garde artist Yoko Ono, much to the dislike of the other three Beatles and their producer George Martin. At the same time, the magic of the songwriting of Paul McCartney began to shine through. This angered John Lennon, and their relationship started going downhill.

In 1967, The Beatles produced the film, *Magical Mystery Tour*, the idea of which was Paul McCartney's, but John also worked on it diligently with Paul, as writer, performer, director and editor. This film showed that The Beatles were together and active. This was a favorite of John Lennon, and *I Am The Walrus* was his favorite track. It was weird, and probably that is why John liked it. The album *Magical Mystery Tour* is very powerful, because of *Strawberry Fields Forever*, *Penny Lane*, and *All You Need Is Love*. Unfortunately, however, Paul McCartney made an unsatisfactory deal with the BBC television network in selling the first rights of *Magical Mystery Tour*. On June 25th, 1967, the BBC asked The Beatles to perform the song, *All You Need Is Love*, and it rose to #1 in both Great Britain and in the U.S.

Both Beatles tunes *I Am the Walrus* and *Strawberry Fields Forever* were influenced by guitar God Jimi Hendrix in 1967. He paid tribute to The Beatles by performing *Sgt. Pepper's Lonely Hearts Club Band*. Paul McCartney later noted on a VH *One-to-One* special, "In the 60s, to have Jimi Hendrix play one of your songs was just the ultimate form of flattery, for us as a band!"

Also in 1967, Brian Epstein had renegotiated The Beatles' appearance contract with Ed Sullivan, to show three new music videos of The Beatles performing their current hits, *Hello Goodbye*, *Strawberry Fields Forever*, and

Penny Lane. Paul McCartney wanted The Beatles to return to touring at any cost. That inspired him to write the song, *Fool On The Hill,* a song that has become a regular feature on his tours.

When in 1968 The Beatles were at the retreat of the Maharishi Mahesh Yogi, they wanted to get back to their Rock 'n' Roll roots. So, they began to write more new songs. All of these songs, which they wrote in Rishikesh, would later be coalesced together on what was called *The Beatles (White Album),* or as it is more popularly known in history as simply *The Beatles' White Album.* This was one of their biggest selling albums to date. Each one of the Beatles was at the peak of his creative power, and the four solo artists united together to make one album, although the group had collapsed. On this album, we see the individual characteristics of The Beatles – John, the radical, Paul, the songsmith, George, the moral, and Ringo, the peace maker. This album went Platinum 19 times in the US. It has got Paul McCartney's famous songs, *Obla-di, Obla-da, I Will,* and *Back In The U.S.S.,* George Harrison's Masterpiece *While My Guitar Gently Weeps,* John Lennon's cleverly titled, *Everybody's Got Something To Hide Except Me And My Monkey,* and Ringo Starr's *Don't Pass Me Bye.* Jim James calls this album a time machine, because different parts speak to different themes, at different times.

During this time, John Lennon was trying to divorce his wife Cynthia and getting closer to Yoko Ono. Paul showed his sympathy to Cynthia and Julian by writing the song, *Hey Jules,* which later became *Hey Jude.*

The Beatles had not produced a hit film since *HELP* in 1965. Both John and Paul felt it would be a good idea to write new songs about jolly British kids who had no apparent direction. *Yellow Submarine,* a 1968 British animated musical fantasy film based on the music of The Beatles, was one such attempt. This script was picked up by Capitol records and United Artists, and released all over the United States. Both Paul and John disagreed with the producers of this film, Hal Bradox and Dick Lester, but, they were forced to compromise by excluding *the Blue Meanies*, in exchange for their new compositions from the album soundtrack. These songs included : *Yellow Submarine*, *Only a Northern Song* (which was written by Harrison), *All Together Now* (written by McCartney with Lennon), *Hey Bulldog* (written by Lennon, with McCartney), *It's All Too Much* (written by Harrison), and *All You Need Is Love* (which all four Beatles sing and play). By this time each of the four Beatles was after pursuing his own personal love and business interests and no longer interested in functioning as a group.

Yellow Submarine is a song about NEMbutles, (which are yellow and submarine shaped). This song was popularized by Ringo Starr. The Beatles were not interested very much in the soundtrack album of the film, and so they included whatever they felt was substandard. Paul McCartney's song, *All Together Now*, on this album, became a hit for children's entertainment.

The Beatles' animated 1968 film *Yellow Submarine* was digitally re-restored and re-released on May 28th 2012 and was shown in movie theaters across the U.S.A. and Canada, at the insistence of Sir Paul McCartney, when the 2012 Grammy Awards were celebrated.

The Beatles produced an excellent album, *Abbey Road* in 1969, after a six-month valiant effort. After this album, they all went their separate ways. *Abbey Road* was The Beatles' final creation as a group. The songs on this album are just excellent. The crowning item on this album is the lyric, "And in the end, the love you take is equal to the love you make!"

Since *Abbey Road* was their final creation as The Beatles, it is necessary to describe it track by track. *Come Together* by John Lennon is the opening track. *Something* by George Harrison is a moving love song. *Maxwell's Silver Hammer* by Paul McCartney is about a serial killer. George Harrison described it this way: "Some people will hate it and some people will really love it!" As usual, John Lennon loathed it.

On *Oh! Darling*, by Paul McCartney, he used a different vocal sound and a macho rhythm. *Octopus's Garden* by Ringo Starr shows that The Beatles were not only artists, but entertainers too. *I Want You (She's So Heavy)* is about Yoko Ono. It is the longest track on this album, and is very complicated. *Here Comes The Sun* is George Harrison's jewel. By 2010, it was their best-selling individual song. *Because* is John Lennon's showcase, where Lennon, Harrison, and McCartney sang about love, drugs, and nature as if they were the same thing. The remaining songs are a medley, rather than separate entities, and serve as the grand finale of this album. The nine songs in this medley are: *You Never Give Me Your Money, Sun King, Mean Mr. Mustard, Polythene Pam, She Came In Through The Bathroom Window, Golden Slumbers, Carry That Weight* and *The End. The End* introduces the band as musicians.

Much of the description of the tracks off *Abbey Road* is from the special edition of Rolling Stone's *The Beatles.*

Both sides of *Abbey Road* end abruptly. By the time the album hit the shelves, The Beatles had disbanded.

When *Abbey Road* was being recorded, Yoko Ono was suffering from a back injury, due to a car crash, but John had to go, reluctantly, because a substantial amount of money was at stake. So, John Lennon ordered a huge bed from the famous British department store, Harrods, and Yoko was right there on the bed during the recording session. Even though she was bed-ridden during the *Abbey Road* sessions, Yoko Ono did not refrain from ordering The Beatles around, by commanding that "Beatles will do this and Beatles will do that!"

Paul became furious with her behavior, and corrected her by asking her to refer to them as "The Beatles", instead of just "Beatles".

Paul McCartney created a beautiful medley from all of the unfinished songs by The Beatles. It was very popular and drove *Abbey Road's* success. John Lennon, however, did not like the medley, and was burning with envy, against Paul. On one night, when Paul had left the studio to enjoy a candlelit supper with Linda, the woman who would later become his wife, John forcibly entered Paul's house and destroyed a painting that he had given to Paul.

The science of imaginary solution known as *Adventures in Pataphysics* by Alfred Jarry, a French dramatist, caught the attention of Paul McCartney and he used it on the album *Abbey Road*.

The medley on the album *Abbey Road* was a glorious achievement by The Beatles, because of Paul McCartney's *You never give me your money*, and *The Love you take is equal to the love you make*, with the perfect concluding phrase for this album, *The End*. These are the best lyrics by Paul McCartney.

Paul tried his best to keep The Beatles together, but after *Abbey Road*, the chance of The Beatles coming together evaporated, and this disappointed the world. A great band was gone forever.

Paul McCartney worked hard to revive the group and *Let It Be,* the last album of The Beatles, was the result. After the success of *Abbey Road,* the idea was to show the world that The Beatles could get their act together and perform ensemble pieces, rather than making records of songs played individually by each Beatle, as had been the case in Abbey Road. They decided to film the sessions because they wanted to show how the whole process worked, but the film just proved it did not work. John Lennon was by this time addicted to hash, absorbed in Yoko Ono and did not care a hoot about anything else. Paul and John had no interest in George Harrison's songs. George left at one point, announcing he was quitting the group after a fight with John Lennon. The Beatles made several attempts to revive themselves as a group, and to rehearse together, but ultimately they compromised on just putting together an album.. The album *Let It Be* was released on May 28th, 1970. It was on the Billboard Hot 100 Album Charts for 59 weeks, and its peek chart position was #1. No matter what happened to The Beatles, the critics liked it.

Let us now describe the individual tracks as in the *Rolling Stone* Special Issue:

Two of Us was not about the friendship of John Lennon and Paul McCartney, but about Paul McCartney and his wife, Linda Eastman.

Across the Universe was by John Lennon and had some of his best lyrics on it, and good poetry.

I Me Mine by George Harrison and was the final song that The Beatles recorded before they broke up.

Dig It by John Lennon was not exactly a song, with Lennon shouting whatever names came into his mind.

Let It Be was about Paul McCartney's dream of his late mother.

Maggie Mae was a folk song about a sailor who was ripped off by a prostitute. John Lennon and Paul McCartney were inspired to write many such songs, while on tour in Hamburg, Germany.

I've Got a Feeling was good proof of what could happen when John Lennon and Paul McCartney collaborated sincerely. That was also true of *One After 909*.

The Long and Winding Road was a piano ballad by Paul McCartney, with Ray Charles in mind. It became #1 in America, and Ray Charles himself recorded it.

Actually, George Harrison had many good solo songs to offer, but somehow the comparatively inferior song *For You Blue* happened to be selected for the album. No wonder George Harrison felt that John Lennon and Paul McCartney were unfair to his best songs.

One of the best songs off this album was *Get Back* by Paul McCartney, which, along with *Don't Let Me Down* were credited to Billy Preston, whom The Beatles first met while on tour in London in 1961.

For Paul, Yoko was a hindrance and for Yoko, Paul was an obstacle. Both of them were trying to make John do what they wanted him to do to complete their visions. Both were very shrewd, but Paul had more talent, experience and famous songs to his credit. Paul was trying to be bossy to all, because he could not see the band collapsing. So, he had to say to Yoko, "Get Back!" Irritated by Paul, George quit the group, but was called back by Paul, and then, when he returned, John and Ringo vehemently objected. In 1970 the break-up of The Beatles shattered the world. John Lennon described it as a divorce. The real reason for The Beatles' break-up could be seen in the film, *Let It Be*. It was a bore, and the group's playing and singing were worse, but because of the strength of Paul's solos, the film received a nomination and a Grammy Award for Best Original Score for a Motion Picture at the 1970 Grammy Awards. Thirty three years later, Paul McCartney remixed it and called it, *Let It Be Naked.* However, the world had gotten used to the original version.

Although The Beatles – the Fab Four - were an entity no more, individual members of the group continued performing, and their songs retained the popularity they had in the 1960s. Many hit songs by The Beatles never made it onto any album. *From Me to You* was a very professional and polished effort by John and Paul. *Thank You Girl* was an expression of gratitude to the females in their audience. *She Loves You* was a best-selling song written by John and Paul.

August 22nd, 2011 saw the sudden death of Jerry Leiber at 78, who, with Mike Stoller, was part of the famous songwriting team, Leiber and Stoller that had written so many of Elvis Presley's songs and also wrote *Kansas City,* which The Beatles had recorded in 1964, as *Kansas City/ Hey-Hey-Hey-Hey!* a version by Little Richard, as a part of a medley of songs that they began performing in their early days in Hamburg, Germany.

In April 2012, Sir Paul McCartney was joined on stage by former Who front-man Roger Daltrey, for a performance of *Carry That Weight/ The End* (the medley from *Abbey Road),* at London's renowned Royal Albert Hall.

Fans continue to attend the sell-out solo performances of Sir Paul McCartney and Ringo Starr in droves, all around the globe. George Harrison performed with Eric Clapton at selected venues in Japan and other locations, before his tragic death in 2001. In addition to this, John Lennon's sons Sean Lennon and Julian Lennon perform to enthusiastic crowds with just the mention of the name of their world-famous father, and with frequent appearances by Yoko Ono Lennon. John's former wife, Cynthia Lennon and George's former wife, Patti Boyd also are often the subjects of mass media adulation by at the annual Fest for Beatles Fans in Chicago and New York.

A famous columnist, Jeff Edelstein, asked in 2011, *"Where are The Beatles when you need them?"* The economic situation was despairing at that time. The stock market was down and the unemployment rate was way up. Corporate Executives were stuffing their own pockets with very large bonuses. The Republicans, and in particular, the members of the Tea Party were opposing the taxation of billionaires and were also trying to remove the legitimate benefits from the poor. Jeff Edelstein remembered The Beatles, who had lightened up the hearts of America, and had raised the human spirit, in similar circumstances in the early 1960s. Unfortunately, Edelstein observed, no such group was visible upon the horizon. His observation underscores not only the strength and power of The Beatles, but the revolutionary nature of their music. The sophistication and innovativeness of their songs provide the key to the sustained success of The Beatles. Their music had a unique style that mesmerized the world and achieved a timeless quality. The Beatles became an inspiration for all succeeding generations of musicians.

"The Beatles are the only group in the history of pop music that is actually better than everyone says they are," Dick Clark told *Life Magazine* in 2012, "Imagine a whole planet feeling like that, 48 years after they fell apart. Their records retain every ounce of raw power. This is not nostalgia. If it were, no one under 50 would listen to their music.

If you take away The Beatles, the whole pack of cards will fall over. Their overwhelming impact created a culture and industry that last long-since outlasted them. If you think that The Rolling Stones or Beyoncé or Skrillex would have even had a chance to exist without The Beatles, you would be wrong. So, think again. The Beatles were the ones who delivered the idea that you could juice up inanimate objects on recordings with your own personality.

Their genius lies in their ability to find the joy in every piece of blank technology.

It is uncertain whether we will ever see the likes of Rock'n'Roll groups of their caliber again. The challenge lies in the fact that no group before or since has ever been able to replicate their level of proficiency".

Many books and newspapers in the last several decades have described in great detail the delirious behavior by fans when The Beatles performed in Chicago, for the first time in September 1964. When Paul McCartney returned to Soldier Field in 1990, the joy of the earlier time was still there and the screams were equally loud, as if the fans had still not gotten over their first bout of Beatlemania.

2

JOHN LENNON,
THE FOUNDER BEATLE

Since childhood, it has been my lifelong desire to visit one day the Beatles' Story Experience Museum in Liverpool, England, and on Saturday, September 25th, 2005 my dream came true.

I had been after my father for many years to take me there, and he finally got the time to take me after he retired as a professor, at The University of Michigan in Ann Arbor. We flew from Detroit to London, aboard British Airways. From London, we boarded the Virgin Trains, which took us on the two and half hour journey to Liverpool. Our taxi driver in Liverpool led us straight to the Albert Docks, where The Beatles Story Experience Museum is located. From there, he led us straight to Mathew Street, which is home to The Cavern Club, where The Beatles were first discovered in 1960. Mathew Street also has a string of shops, devoted to Beatles memorabilia. Each year, millions of devoted Beatles fans, like me, from all over the world, come to pay homage to a bronze statue of The Fab Four. I even met one man, from Sadashiv

Peth, Pune, Maharashtra, India who was a visitor to the museum.

The magic of this museum is that it helps to recapture the innocence of a momentous era in popular music history, known simply as BEATLEMANIA, for future generations, as well as those who were fortunate enough to be present when The Beatles first arrived on the world stage in the early 1960s and then continued to dominate the billboard charts, and create an insurmountable frenzy that would last for many decades to come.

The story begins with an audio guided tour by John Lennon's sister, Julia, who describes how in 1957, the barely fifteen-year-old Paul McCartney met seventeen-year-old John Lennon, at a social at St. Peter's Church Hall in Liverpool, England. This started a musical partnership that transcended generations, and changed the course of the history of popular music forever.

John (Winston) Lennon had a distinct personality. He was a member of the group, but was also different from the others in many ways. He was born on October 9, 1940 in Liverpool, England. His father was an Irish Merchant Seaman, who, at the start of World War II, abandoned his family. John's mother, Julia, took care of John, until 1958, when she was killed in a car accident. After that, it was his Aunt Mimi who looked after him.

John was disruptive in school, and when he was expelled for his misbehavior, he was enrolled in the famous Quarry Bank High School. Nobody at that time could have imagined the musical revolution that was in the teenager's future. John formed his first skiffle group in 1957, with Pete Shotton, Eric Griffiths, Bill Smith, Len Garry, and Colin Hanton. The group earlier was called The Blackjacks. Then, the name of the group was changed to The Quarrymen, Johnny and the Moondogs, and then Long John and the Silver Beetles.

When John Lennon met Paul McCartney for the first time at the church social, John Lennon was impressed with Paul's ability to play Eddie Cochran's *Twenty Flight Rock* on the guitar – and the fact that he knew all the words. Paul was impressed that John had his own skiffle band, and played rhythm guitar. Paul was left-handed, and so he had to play the guitar backwards (upside-down). The good first impression of McCartney's performance led to an invitation from John to join his band, The Quarrymen.

John and Paul used to miss school and go into the fields and practice for hours on songs by their American Rock'n'Roll idols, such as Buddy Holly, Chuck Berry, the Everly Brothers, Little Richard, Fats Domino, Carl Perkins, Jerry Lee Lewis, and of course, "the King" - Elvis Presley. The impact of Elvis Presley on John Lennon started when John heard '*Heartbreak Hotel*' in 1956. This marked his initiation to Rock 'n' Roll. He used to listen to Elvis songs, and twang his guitar constantly and stomp his feet while playing. Little Richard (Penniman) had a collection of American records, and so John made friends with him and visited his home.

The Beatles were successful, because they transformed American pop, after bringing it from America to England, and then made it popular back in America. They recognized the best aspects of American music, and had the ability to transform it and exploit it. John Lennon was the architect of this successful endeavor. John Lennon released 13 albums with The Beatles, and 13 on his own. He also acted in films and wrote poetry, and was an artist too.

John Lennon met his future love and wife, Yoko Ono, at the Indica Art Gallery in London, in 1966. Her father came from a very sophisticated and educated family, and had a job in the United States. Therefore, Yoko had her schooling in the United States, and was sufficiently acquainted with the Western culture. Smoking, drinking, and an early interest in sex, were not taboo to her. Though she wanted to become an opera singer, she had no musical ability. But, she had such a high opinion of herself that she thought she could achieve anything that she desired. She dropped out of college and became a rebel. She met in the U.S.A, a very good student, Toshi Ichiyanagi. He was an accomplished person and he won several prizes for his musical compositions. Yoko married him, but she was a dominant wife. She wanted to be treated like a queen by Toshi. She was very selfish, and she spent money as she pleased. Her sexual behavior was irresponsible, and she had to undergo many illegal abortions. So, in 1962, her parents dispatched her back to Tokyo. She became severely depressed and Toshi had to institutionalize her.

One day, Toshi introduced her to a man from New York, Tony Cox. He was a dangerous person and had underground Mafia connections. She married Tony Cox illegally, because she was already married. To make things legal, she had to divorce Tony first, and then divorce her husband, Toshi, and then remarry Tony. She had a daughter, Kyoko, from that marriage. Finally, she came to New York in 1964. Until then, The Beatles were unknown to her. She claimed she was an avant-garde artist, and wanted to sell her art to Paul McCartney, but Paul was too clever to fall for it, and he sent her to John Lennon, who had a fascination for the avant-garde.

When John met Yoko, he was so fascinated by her that he felt like leaving his band mates. They became of no interest to him. John's first wife, Cynthia Lennon, did not see any utility in fighting, because she knew that he was never really hers, but John and Yoko had that unity of body and mind, with each other. In 1969, John Lennon and Yoko Ono married.

In the early years of their marriage, John and Yoko had several marital disputes, and they even were living separately for some time. During their separation, John lived in Los Angeles for a while with May Pang. She was a very pretty 22-year-old, Chinese-American. She had a very positive influence on John, and was very unselfish. She has written a book called, ***Loving John***, about this period. During the time he was with May Pang, John Lennon released his solo album, *Shaved Fish*, which included, *Cold Turkey, Instant Karma, Power To The People, Happy Christmas (War Is Over), Give Peace a Chance* and *Imagine.*

Finally, John and Yoko ended their separation. John had to entreat Yoko for that. They both had changed during this period of separation. John had gotten rid of his bad traits, such as drunkenness, jealousy, possessiveness, and sexual problems. But, he was still insecure and self-doubting. They became better friends.

Their son, Sean (Taro), was born on October 9, 1975 when John was 35 and Yoko 42. John became a proud parent. Elton John was Sean's Godfather. Elton and John were good friends. In fact, in 1974, they had a show at Madison Square Garden, on Thanksgiving Day, November 28th. They sang, *I Saw Her Standing There, Lucy in the Sky with Diamonds,* and *Whatever Gets You Thru the Night.* John Lennon later recorded *Whatever Gets You Thru the Night* with Elton John at the world famous Hit Factory recording studio.

When The Beatles returned from Rishikesh, India, John and Yoko became active in Anti-Vietnam War campaigns. In November, 1969, John returned his M.B.E. medal, as a protest against the Vietnam War. At this time, John and Yoko released their album *Live Peace in Toronto 1969*. The magazine *Rolling Stone* named John Lennon as the Man of the Year, and the BBC broadcast a television special, *"The World of John Lennon and Yoko Ono"*. None of the other Beatles were involved in these activities.

In 1970, John wanted to hold a huge Peace Festival in Montreal, but he could not get the permission from the City Council. He and Yoko had to satisfy themselves with only a message of support to the 8,000 gathered in a nuclear disarmament rally in London.

John Lennon was very public about his feelings about war and peace. His activities included many benefit concerts, appearances on the Dick Cavett and David Frost TV shows, and co-hosting the *Mike Douglas Show*. He was also active in the protest over the Attica State Prison riots. On January 30, 1972, when British Soldiers shot 13 people of Ireland, John responded with the songs, *Sunday Bloody Sunday*, *Keep Ireland for The Irish*, *Put the English Back to Sea*, and *The Luck of the Irish*. Obviously, the British people did not like these activities of John.

Later John and Yoko released the album *Sometime in New York City*. This album had protest songs like *Angela*, *Sunday Bloody Sunday*, *The Luck of The Irish*, and *Woman is the Nigger of the World*.

John had to struggle hard to get a Permanent Residence Visa in the U.S. Because of his active part in opposing the Vietnam War, he was on President Nixon's enemy list. The F.B.I. director, J.Edgar Hoover, was harassing John and Yoko. Their apartment was constantly under surveillance. In fact, at one stage, they were to be deported, but, due to massive public support, a signature campaign, the backing of The *New York Times* and New York Mayor Lindsay's appeal to the Immigration Authorities, the Deportation order was cancelled. Ultimately, after his lawyer's efforts, John got a Permanent Residence Visa in 1976, and then John, Yoko and Sean went to Japan in 1977. He was greeted by the Immigration Officer there, with a "Welcome Home, Mr. Lennon!" and John was thrilled.

On this Japanese trip, John saw an old photograph of Yoko's great-grand father Zenjiro Yasuda. He was a celebrity, musician, and poet. He was the Emperor's banker. It was a strange coincidence that John and Zenjiro had the same birth date, similar careers, and a likeness in their appearances. John remarked that probably, in a former life, he had been Zenjiro, and Yoko asked him not to say that, because Zenjiro was assassinated. She, of course, had no idea that there would be a similarity between Zenjiro and John in this respect, too. On this Japanese trip, Sean saw *Yellow Submarine* on TV. He ran to his daddy, and asked him, "Daddy, were you a Beatle?"

John Lennon sometimes had cheap, vulgar and bizarre desires. Yoko Ono was also a partner in this. They made a public spectacle of themselves, by depicting their naked pictures on the cover of their album, *Two Virgins*. There was no music on it, some inaudible words, and some footstep noise. His excuse for his bizarre behavior was, "I can't be a good Beatle all the time." John had produced some obscene, erotic lithographs of Yoko and exhibited them in several London art galleries.

John and Paul were drifting apart very much during this time. Each hated the other's spouse. Their telephone talks were vitriolic. John Lennon was very much jealous of Paul McCartney. John used to ask Yoko, "What magical facilities does Paul have that I do not?"

The Beatles gradually found success in their own individual endeavors. In an attempt to bury past hostilities, John invited Paul and Linda to his Santa Monica residence. They spent this time together singing some old songs like, *Please Please Me* and *Ticket To Ride*. Spending time together in New York, they went to the famous upper east side restaurant, Elaine's, together. However, when they could find nothing on the menu that they liked, they ordered a pizza to be brought in from outside. Elaine's swallowed her anger, as the guests were so renowned.

Starting in 1975, John and Yoko began living a life of retirement. There were no new albums, no new singles, and no new idiosyncrasies. However, John gave interviews to the magazines *Playboy*, *Rolling Stone* and to the B.B.C radio network. John and Yoko's life together lasted longer than John's life with The Beatles. There was a perception in the mind of the public – and there was some truth in it – that The Beatles split when Yoko came on the scene. This hurt John.

On the fateful, foggy night of December 8, 1980 night, when John and Yoko were returning to their apartment, a psychopath, Mark David Chapman, fired five shots, killing John instantaneously. He joined the famous group of the Kennedys, Martin Luther King, Mahatma Gandhi and Trotsky, who had been assassinated earlier. The killer had a copy of John and Yoko's album *Double Fantasy*, which John had autographed earlier.

The news of John Lennon's assassination reverberated throughout the world. John Lennon was an honest, but cynical person. The music of The Beatles in general and John Lennon in particular has received appreciation from generation after generation. Lennon's songs were popular because they were personal and touched the heart.

Paul McCartney was like a brother to John – in good times and bad. John's death was a bitter and cruel blow to him. He described Chapman as "the jerk of all jerks". *Here Today*, a song by Paul McCartney, is a personal tribute to John, and Paul makes it a point to sing it on all his tours. George Harrison was stunned by the news, and he suffered his grief alone by retreating to his mansion in England. Ringo Starr went to New York and met Yoko.

John's son Sean was only five years old when John was assassinated. John was a kind and loving father to Sean. He played with him, and taught Sean to swim. They watched television together. Sean is now a professional musician in his own right. He has preserved precious memories of his father in his heart. He loves his mother Yoko very much and they both have kept John's legacy alive.

John's first wife Cynthia and son Julian also went to New York to offer their condolences.

The famous TV journalist and anchor-woman Barbara Walters interviewed Chapman in 1992, in jail. Chapman told Barbara that Satan entered into him and made him commit this senseless act.

We can only speculate what might have been were it not for that chilly December night in 1980, when Lennon and Ono had merely stepped out of their limousine, and were jolted suddenly by the sound of what sounded like fire crackers. If John Lennon had not been killed, he would have been 70 years old on October 9, 2010. Yoko commemorated the anniversary day by re-issuing all of his solo albums. *Double Fantasy: Stripped Down* is the most prominent in this collection. Some other albums are *Gimme Some Truth, Power To The People*, the hits, *Plastic Ono*

Band, Imagine, Mind Games, Walls And Bridges, Rock'n'Roll and *Milk and Honey.*

Yoko Ono improved the quality of these albums by eliminating the extraneous instruments' effects and some echo. As a result, the listeners are impressed by the quality of John's singing and his diction.

Memorials for John Lennon

PBS broadcast a documentary, *Lennon NYC*, describing John Lennon's life in New York City, when he disconnected himself from The Beatles.

The UK Independent movie, *Nowhere Boy*, described John Lennon's teen years in Liverpool. Yoko Ono released a collection of all of John's eight albums and much more in *Signature Box: John Lennon.* She modified and edited the versions of his original songs.

Thousands of Lennon fans gathered in Central Parks' noted region Strawberry Fields, and honored the legend, John Lennon on what would have been his 70th birthday. His music is eloquent to all, irrespective of their nationality or age. Yoko Ono awarded the Annual Lennon Ono Grant for Peace. Also, Yoko Ono lit the Annual Tower for Peace in Reykjavik, Iceland, in John Lennon's honor and memory. John Lennon has become immortal in his death, and continues to inspire the new generations.

Remembrances

John Lennon's assassination produced a sea of reactions by his friends and admirers.

This is what Rolling Stone's, Jann S. Wenner had to say about John Lennon:

"Probably there is no single figure more important in the history of Rock & Roll than John Lennon. He didn't invent it; nor did he embody it in that towering way that Elvis or Chuck Berry did, but he did more than anyone else to move it forward and give it a conscience. As a Beatle, he helped shape the agenda of the sixties, socially and politically, no less than musically. As a solo artist, John made music that disturbed, and soothed, and provoked, and saw community. As a human being, he was an exemplar of honesty. His was not an untroubled life, but he never dishonored his art; he never glossed over his pain, nor did he ever temper a strongly held belief. His impact remains universal, and his impact is undiminished. Many of his post-Beatle compositions – Give Peace a Chance, Instant Karma, Imagine – have rightly become international Rock 'n' Roll anthems. They were born out of tough-minded realism; they have got a cosmic epiphany, and a hard-won idealism".

The magazine *John Lennon Remembered* says, "John found love and surrendered to it when he met Yoko Ono. Their relationship endured challenges from within and without, and they became one of the most touching and mythical of twentieth-century romances. They were gallant in doing what were in effect performance – art pieces, records, bed-ins, bag-ins, happenings, billboards that read WAR IS OVER IF YOU WANT IT, as they went to spread their message of peace. In the end, although John was a complicated man, he chose to uncomplicate his art, to figure out his life, and in the process, he merged the two. It broke our hearts the day he died. He touched and enriched my life very deeply – personally, professionally, and spiritually. For the world of music and the world we live in, we are all forever in your debt, John Lennon."

Relying heavily on The Collector's Edition of *Uncut – 25 Years on …. John Lennon Remembered*, I will mention a few reactions to John's tragic assassination. Andy Newmark, a drummer, was so psychologically affected by Lennon's death that he didn't do anything for six months but lie on a couch. Only Prozac helped him. According to him, John was a confident, authoritative and focused person and The Beatles' work was the ultimate.

The folk group, The Mamas and the Papas were obsessed with John Lennon and were impressed by John's rhythmic guitar. Peter Tork of The Monkees described John as a warrior who went down fighting. Chris Frantz of The Talking Heads remarked that John Lennon represented the artistic and the romantic side of Rock 'n' Roll and had a profound depth of feeling. May Pang, a one-time lover of John, was so shocked that her whole body went cold, when she heard the news.

Jim Sclavunos of the Bad Seeds said that "Lennon's *Give Peace a Chance* made the U.S. government panic. There were many disciples like Dee Snyder who loved him so much that she felt the statement "The Beatles are bigger than Jesus", as said by Lennon, was not off-base, but "really the f *** ing truth". Ozzy Osbourne, the heavy metal super star, admired Lennon, because he stood for his own values in talking about justice and freedom.

Bob Mould of Husker Du thought that Lennon was great because his songs hit a nerve. Phil Manzanera of Roxy Music is of the opinion that Lennon's powerful words and voice have become his lasting legacy. Billy Idol of Generation X thinks that Lennon's tracks like *Cold Turkey* and *Instant Karma* were absolute killers. Damon Gough (Badly Drawn Boy) admired John Lennon because he made a serious attempt to change the world and he pulled it off too. Howe Gelb (Giant Sand) is of the opinion that there has been no one else like Lennon, before or since. Harley (Cockney Rebel) says, "The Beatles impact on fashion, music, attitude, and politics was immeasurable." Bernard Butler (Suede, The Tears) thinks that John Lennon's *Imagine* is a powerful song, so innocent and simplistic.

John Lennon affected and touched many people. He was a visionary. He was no saint, but was committed to telling the truth. His flaws made him seem more human and approachable. He gave the world a life-changing flow of verse and delivery. He may have been vitriolic, but he was also sentimental. He may have been sarcastic, but what he said was powerful.

John and Yoko's plan for 1980

In January 1980, John Lennon and Yoko Ono had announced that they were to embark on a World Tour from December 1980 to 1981. He and Yoko Ono had set up their new version of their Plastic Ono Band, and were set to tour arenas all across the U.S. and then later that same year to Europe. The tour was set to feature re-edited versions of *I Want to Hold Your Hand* and *Watching the Wheels.* There was even a set date for December at the Pontiac Silverdome in Pontiac, Michigan. All this was planned, before that fateful eve of December 8th, 1980. John Lennon had even speculated to reporters that he and the three other ex-Beatles could possibly reunite in the upcoming years.

With the help of then New York Mayor Ed Koch, and Gordon J. Davis, the New York City Parks Commissioner, a special triangular area of Central Park was officially named, Strawberry Fields in honor of John Lennon. This area is often called an "island", because it is conveniently located on Central Park West at the West 72nd Street entrance to Central Park, right near The Dakota, where John and Yoko lived.

In an exclusive letter that was published in the *New York Times*, and in several prominent newspapers on August 19 and 22nd, 1981, John Lennon's widow said that she would pay for whatever plants were needed for the area that were not donated from Lennon fans around the world. Yoko Ono further said that, "It happens to be where John and I took our last walk together. John would be glad that this was given to him, an island named after his song, rather than a statue or a monument."

Each year on October 9th and December 8th, several hundreds of devoted John Lennon/Beatles fans come to this special circle overlooking Central Park and the Dakota Apartment building, where Yoko Ono still lives, to celebrate the life of their *Working Class Hero*, John Winston (Ono) Lennon.

In 1991, a special light Tower for Peace was created by Yoko Ono in Reykjavik, Iceland to mark the 10th Anniversary of John Lennon's death. In 1996, a John Lennon Memorial Museum was opened to the general public.

Since that awful day, Yoko Ono has dedicated her life to promote to the world, the lasting memory of John Lennon.

In 2007, a special album which was entitled, *Instant Karma: The Amnesty International Campaign to Save Darfur* was released in both the U.S and in the U.K. This album is a compilation of John Lennon songs sung by various artists, including George Harrison's son Dhani, to benefit Amnesty International's campaign.

In 2012, Yoko Ono was invited to the famous Vadehra Art Gallery in New Delhi, India, to organize a special exhibition "Our Beautiful Daughters". Its theme was gender empowerment.

Highlights of John Lennon's famous Interview

John Lennon granted an interview to David Sheff in 1980. Yoko Ono was also with him. It was his last Interview before he was killed. It covers a lot of territory. It is a fascinating piece of work. David Sheff asked sympathetic questions. This very interesting interview gives an insight into John Lennon's mind, and shows how strongly opinionated he was. A gist of this Interview is presented here in this separate chapter. His opinions about Paul McCartney and the other Beatles bring out John Lennon's ego and jealousy of Paul.

Speaking about himself, John Lennon said that he never went to see Elvis, but he worshipped him, because he knew that without Elvis, there would be no Beatles. In the interview, John said that The Beatles were more intellectual, but frankly their basic appeal was their music. John further said that, he confined himself to his apartment, in later years, because he did not want to be repetitive like Picasso and live on his laurels. He added that The Beatles wanted to live together and work together, but when it was hard to do so, they stepped out, and he wasn't interested in writing something every six months like Paul.

John was of the opinion that the world thinks of itself as divided into races and countries, but really it is only just one world. A lot more can happen, when you aren't doing anything, than when you appear to be doing something.

Did John listen to his own records? His reply was, "Not for pleasure, but for revising and remixing."

About The Beatles' split, he said he needed his space for thinking, but none of The Beatles suffered because of that. John never thought that their separating was like a good thing coming to an end, because The Beatles were young and several years of productivity were still there. When John was asked why he and the other Beatles will not leave aside their personal feelings and come together for a charity concert, he said such concerts are rip-offs and so he had decided to help from what he earns.

John became very angry when the interviewer asked him about the chance that he was under Yoko's spell. People put the blame on Yoko. A lot of painful stuff was thrown at John and Yoko. The Society wanted The Beatles to get back together again. A girl once asked Lennon, "When are you going back with The Beatles?" and John cryptically answered, "When are you going back to high school?"

John Lennon freed himself physically from The Beatles, but not mentally. Once he found Yoko, he said the boys were of no interest to him, whatsoever. He said, "You cannot get back together what no longer exists," Even so, John thought The Beatles were the best before anyone else had even heard of them. About his relationship with Yoko, he described it as a teacher, pupil relationship, he being the pupil. Yoko expanded on this and said that women have inner wisdom; men never develop the inner wisdom, and so men rely on women. John often referred to Yoko as Mother Superior.

Even so, Lennon and Yoko Ono held a concert to raise money for the treatment of retarded children. This event was held on August 30th, 1972 at Madison Square Garden in New York. Sha-na-na, Stevie Wonder, and the Wonder

Love were other participants. The band Elephant's Memory, was backing them. John Lennon's rhythms were still strong and he exhibited a great amount of energy. He proved that he was still a great performer, and had taken a new direction in his music. All the groups sang together, *Give Peace a Chance*. *Woman Is the Nigger of the World*, a notorious song, was also an attraction of this event. *Come Together* and *Mother*, two passionate songs were greeted with a strong, enthusiastic reaction from the young spectators. Sha-na-na was also delightful and Stevie Wonder was too.

John Lennon loved Sean so much that he would talk about him forever. Sean was his biggest pride, because he and Yoko had to try very hard to have him. The doctors thought he and Yoko would never have a child, because Yoko was too old, and John had abused his health. But, a Chinese doctor put them on a strong regimen, and it succeeded.

John's son Julian, from his first marriage, didn't have good relations with his father, but they were in communication. Yoko's daughter from her first marriage, Kyoko, was separated from her, because Tony Cox, Yoko's first husband, took her away. She finally got custody of her from the courts.

Many historians want to analyze The Beatles Phenomenon and the personalities of The Beatles, but John thought that it was all irrelevant. At one time in the interview, John said that The Beatles talk bored him to death. He further added that The Beatles did enough and that people should not expect any more from them.

In the interview, John gave his reactions to almost all of the Beatles' songs. We will briefly summarize this, because John's thoughts and opinions are illuminating and it also provides a list of some important songs by The Beatles.

Strawberry Fields (Forever): Lennon wrote it and gave it to George Harrison to sing. George was not a good singer at that time, but he improved since then. It was because of Lennon that Ringo and George got a piece of John and Paul's songwriting. But, John regretted that they didn't give any recognition to him.

In the early days, the majority of the singles in the movies were John's. Then he became self-conscious, and Paul started dominating the group. When it came to their fans, it was obvious that he had more male following and Paul had more female following. He further added that Ringo was a "damn good drummer" and Paul was "the most innovative bass player".

All My Loving was a damn good piece of work by Paul.

Little Child was written for Ringo by Paul and John.

Hold Me Tight John felt was a poor song by Paul.

I Wanna Be Your Man was a song given by Paul and John to Mick Jagger and Keith Richards of The Rolling Stones.

I'll Keep You Satisfied and *Love of the Loved* were both by Paul.

I'm in Love, was by John.

Can't Buy Me Love, From a Window and *Like Dreamers Do* were completely Paul's.

And I Love Her was by Paul for the film, "*A Hard Day's Night*".

I'll Be Back was completely by John.

One and One is Two was one of Paul's bad attempts.

I Feel Fine and *No Reply* were John's.

Eight Days a Week was a lousy song by John and Paul.

It's Only Love was John's and was lousy.

We Can Work it out shows the optimism of Paul, but 'Life is very short and there's no time' shows John's attitude.

Norwegian Wood was about one of John's affairs.

Here, There and Everywhere by Paul was one of John's favorite songs.

Yellow Submarine was Paul's inspiration, Paul's idea and Paul's title, but sang by Ringo.

For No One was a nice piece of work by Paul and was John's favorite.

Got To Get You Into My Life was one of Paul's best songs, which describes Paul's experience of taking acid.

With a Little Help from My Friends was Paul's with a little help from John. Ringo sang it and he was introduced by Paul, as the one and only Billy Shears.

When I'm Sixty Four was again completely by Paul. John Lennon said, "I would never even dream of writing a song like that."

Baby, You're a Rich Man was a combination of two separate pieces, one by Paul and the other by John.

I am the Walrus - The first line was written when John was on an acid trip and the second line was written on another acid trip, during the next weekend.

Magical Mystery Tour was Paul's concept.

Within You, Without You was George's best song and shows his innate talent.

Hey Jude was one of Paul's masterpieces about John's son Julian. Paul was like an uncle to him. John thought that Paul was always good with kids.

Revolution was completely by John depicting The Beatles' position on the Vietnam War and Revolution. John Lennon did this in spite of Brian Epstein's admonition.

Back in the U.S.S.R was based on the Chuck Berry song, *Back in the U.S.A.* and was completely by Paul.

Happiness Is a Warm Gun was completely by John; it was not about drugs. Some of it had sexual connotations and some of it was about happiness after imagining that he had shot somebody.

Rocky Raccoon and *Why Don't We Do It In The Road* were by Paul.

Julia was again by John, a sort of combination of Yoko and John's mother, written in India.

Birthday was by both John and Paul, but was a piece of garbage.

When asked about his favorite albums, John said, "I like different songs from different albums, but no particular album." However, John said he likes: *Pepper, The White Album, Revolver, Rubber Soul* and *Please Please Me.*

Me and My Monkey was about John and Yoko, when they were in the glow of love. John used to call Yoko Ono as "Mother Superior".

Sexy Sadie was John's last song, before he left India with a bad taste about the Maharishi. The Maharishi was a father figure. Lennon's views about such father figures were very honest and practical. He said, "People give them the right to give them a recipe for life, and then, instead of the truth, people begin to look at the person who brings the message."

Across the Universe was an artsy-fartsy song when Yoko was irritating him. Paul destroyed this great song subconsciously with the lousy track, but the song was great and the words were inspirational.

Nowhere Man and *In My Life* were two songs for which John had to struggle. *There's a Place* had the usual Lennon things: "In my mind, there's no sorrow; It's all in your mind."

This Boy and *All I've Got to Do* were two Smokey Robinson-type songs by John.

I Saw Her Standing There was a good job by Paul.

Tip of My Tongue was Paul's, but John thought that it was garbage.

You Can't Do That was by John.

Don't Want to See You Again was by Paul.

John helped Paul on *I'm Down*.

The Night Before was by Paul, and didn't mean a dam thing.

I Should Have Known Better was by John, and didn't mean a dam thing either.

Don't Bother Me and *I'm Happy Just to Dance with You* were by George.

When I Get Home was by John again, and had a Motown Sound.

I'm a Loser was by John.

Another Girl, Fixing a Hole, I'm Looking Through You, I've Just Seen a Face and *That Means A lot* were all by Paul.

I Don't Want to Spoil the Party was by John, and *Yes It Is* was also.

You've Got to Hide Your Love Away was a Dylany song by John, written in the spirit "If Elvis can do it; If the Everly Brothers can do it, Paul and I can do it too."

Lovely Rita 'was by Paul. There really was no Rita. Paul made her up. John was not interested in writing such third-party songs, but liked to write about himself.

Girl was by John. The dream girl Yoko had not come by that time.

Sgt. Pepper was by Paul. Paul wanted to put some distance between the public and the Beatles and created *Sgt. Pepper*.

Rain was by John- it was the first backward take on any record, anywhere.

Hello, Goodbye, Your Mother Should Know, Fool on the Hill, Step Inside Love and *Ob-la-Di, Ob-la-Da* were by Paul.

Dear Prudence was a song about Mia Farrow's sister, who was in Maharishi's Ashram with The Beatles and was in a hurry to reach God quicker than anybody else.

I'm Only Sleeping was one of John's favorites.

Glass Onion was by John, wherein he had written the line – The Walrus was Paul. *The Continuing Story of Bungalow Bill* was about a guy in the Maharishi's Ashram.

I'm So Tired, a common phrase, was one of John's favorite tracks.

Yer Blues was written by John, in India, while trying to reach God and while feeling suicidal. *Mother Nature's Son* was by Paul, and was based on a lecture by the Maharishi.

Helter Skelter was by Paul completely, and concerned the notorious Charles Manson's stuff, about the massacre he did.

Good Night was written by John for Julian.

Beautiful Boy was written for Sean.

The Ballad of John and Yoko was a folk song and John wrote it in Paris on their Honeymoon.

Come Together' was a funny, bluesy, favorite Beatle track of John, based on Tim Leary's expression "Come Together".

Lady Madonna, All Together Now and *Get Back* were by Paul. John remarked that Paul used to look at Yoko, whenever he sang, "Get back to where you once belonged"!

Let It Be was again by Paul, but John had no clue about what Paul was thinking when he wrote that.

Oh! Darling was a great one of Paul's, but he did not sing it well. John said, "If Paul had any sense, he should have let me sing it."

She Came in through the Bathroom Window was by Paul. That was when they both met Linda for the first time. Maybe Linda came in through the window!

Mean Mr. Mustard, Sun King, Dig a Pony, Surprise, Surprise (Sweet Bird Of Paradox), (off the 1974 John Lennon solo album *Walls And Bridges*) were all pieces of garbage, according to Paul.

Polythene Pam was by John and was about a girl who was dressed in polythene.

Golden Slumber, Carry That Weight and *The End* were all by Paul.

The line in the song *The End* - "And in the end, the love you take is equal to the love you make" triggered Paul to make the caustic remark, "If Paul wants to, he can think."

Hey Bulldog was also by John.

Don't Let Me Down was about Yoko, by John.

You Know My Name (Look Up the Number) was a comedy record by Paul.

The Word was written by both John and Paul together, during their marijuana period.

When the subject of the album Rock 'N' Roll came up, John said, "Yoko was a lot smarter than I, a lot more intelligent and she was always right. But she didn't need to remind me of it over and over".

On the album cover of *Two Virgins*, John and Yoko are shown naked, and it caused a bit of a stir. People got upset by it and called John and Yoko recluses. John thought peoples' reaction was insane. They did this only because they had made love for the first time, and they were just being funny!

The *Plastic Ono Band* was an album by John and Yoko. It was an intriguing thing. It was just a conceptual band, or just an idea.

John admitted he was a very insecure, jealous, possessive male, when he wrote the song, *Jealous Guy,* and also admitted that he wanted to express even his most painful emotions publicly. He thought that praise was never enough, but criticism was always a bit deep.

John resented Paul, and feeling vicious, he wrote the song. *How Do You Sleep?*

Oh Yoko! was one of John's greatest songs, but it never made #1.

In the middle of the night, and *I call your name* expressed a message to Yoko.

Imagine was inspired by a prayer book, which was given to Yoko, and also by Yoko's book, **Grapefruit.** John admits that he was selfish, and did not give Yoko any credit for that.

About *I'm the Greatest,* John thought it was perfect for Ringo to sing. If Ringo sang it, people would not get upset, but if he sang it, they would.

About Lennon/McCartney songs in general, John said that there was an agreement between him and Paul to put both their names on their songs, no matter whether John alone wrote it or Paul alone wrote it, or both.

Woman Is the Nigger of the World, a powerful statement by Yoko in 1968, was turned into a song by John.

Julian was playing drums when John sang, *Ya Ya.* It was hard on Julian to be John Lennon's kid, but John was confident that Julian would deal with it, as he was a clever boy.

When asked about the song *Cold Turkey,* John said that it was self-explanatory - "They thought that I was promoting heroin" - and added that, "We weren't looking at the cause of the drug problem. Why a person needs to take them is important, not who is selling it, and to whom, on a street corner."

About the song, *Instant Karma,* John said that the idea for this song was like instant coffee, presenting something old in a new form.

Happy Xmas (War Is Over) was written together by both John and Yoko. Its message was "WAR IS OVER! (If You Want It)".

What You Got and Bless You were both about Yoko. The former conveyed the message that "You really don't know what you have got till you lose it." Mick Jagger of The Rolling Stones turned, *Bless You* into *Miss You* and it became a hit song.

Don't Worry, Kyoko was Yoko's way of communicating with Kyoko, because she wasn't allowed to see Kyoko (Yoko's daughter from her first marriage).

I'm Moving On was a very powerful song, in the same thought process of John's feeling that he had "had enough" and was "moving on". The song wasn't about any certain feeling in particular, but just that he liked everything simple and straight forward.

This interview took 20 hours of tape. Both John and Yoko were pleased with it. John thought "It will be the reference book".

The final interview session was held on September 28th, 1980 and John was shot dead on December 8, 1980. The interviewer, David Scheff, did not get a chance to talk to John Lennon in between. This interview has been called historic, compassionate and definitive by the Library Guild. The New York Times Book review described it as "A fascinating, detailed glimpse into the workings of a musical genius. A valuable piece of work".

Yoko Ono

The life of Yoko Ono, before she married John Lennon and after, until John died has been described in the chapter on John Lennon. This chapter describes in brief, her present activities, since the tragic death of John Lennon.

Yoko Ono is a talented artist who likes to go beyond the traditional boundaries of sculpture, painting, and music. She had a creative influence on the present and new generation.

Since 2000, she has received many awards for her exhibitions, Yes Yoko Ono. She also installed the Imagine Peace billboard works in New York and around the world. In 2003, she performed Cut Peace in Paris, and in 2004, Ono Called in Open Asia. In 2007, Yoko Ono's Odyssey of a Cockroach was exhibited in Moscow. Also, she organized her Imagine Peace Tower in Reykjavik, Iceland. She got an award for her distinguished body of work from the 2008 College Art Association. Paul McCartney himself sent Yoko Ono a brief note congratulating her on this achievement.

Lord Grade's company, ATV, held the rights for The Beatles' Northern Songs. The company was in trouble, because of their movie, Raise the Titanic. Lord Grade was ready to sell the catalog to Paul McCartney for 20 million pounds, but Yoko did not cooperate and then Michael Jackson snatched the rights from under Paul's nose. Paul, George, and Ringo never liked Yoko. She was as much an embarrassment to The Beatles, as Fergie (the Duchess of York), was to the British Royal Family.

After John's death, gradually, Yoko Ono succeeded in securing her own identity, separate from her celebrity husband. The movies, *Cut Peace*, and *The Bottoms* were instrumental in this. Even so, financially Yoko's efforts did not succeed very well. There was no demand for what she was doing. Many people still thought that she was "the personification of evil".

Yoko Ono tried in vain many different gimmicks to keep herself in the public eye. She exhibited in Los Angeles bronze casts of Lennon's bullet-ridden shirt, and replicas of his shattered glasses. They fetched large amounts of money for her.

Many critics are of the opinion that Yoko Ono used John Lennon as leverage to further her own interests.

Alan Clayson (with Barb Junger and Rob Johnson) has written an excellent biography of Yoko Ono. Its title is Woman – The Incredible Life of Yoko Ono. He has given a critical appraisal of all the post – Lennon albums and music and art of Yoko Ono. Though he is critical of Yoko as a woman, he reassesses Yoko's music and praises its merit and artistic value. The longevity of her work is evidence enough of the quality of her albums. They may not be commercially successful, but they are aesthetically good. Her films are recognized as good work and inspire video artists.

In spite of all the misunderstandings that she created about herself, it can now be said that she has received recognition. She collaborated with young musicians and remixes of her associates to express her vocalizations and experiences. Recently, in 2013, Yoko Ono celebrated her 80th birthday with some of her closest friends and family in the foyer of the Volksbuhne theatre in Berlin. Sean Lennon was very much active in this concert.

Yoko inspired John to be more adventurous and to push back the boundaries of his art. Yoko was not just a partner, but his equal in many ways, and also a teacher. John used to call her as his "Mother Superior". John and

Yoko depended heavily on each other. She was his soul mate, and he was her real man. It must be admitted that Yoko is a courageous woman, who, against all odds, rose to the top in an alien, hostile culture and society.

The John Lennon and Yoko Ono Bed-In for Peace

The John Lennon and Yoko Ono Bed-In for Peace, (regarding the Vietnam War), was held at the Amsterdam Hilton, and also at the Queen Elizabeth Hotel in Montreal (British Columbia, Canada) from May 26th to June 5th, 1969.

What can Asian Indians learn from the Bed-In for Peace? John Lennon had a vision, and it was this vision that he held on to, until his untimely death in 1980. Michael Archer wrote in the "Guardian", (a widely read newspaper in the U.K.), "John Lennon's peace activism allowed the 'hairy hedonists' to propose an alternative attitude to the active resistance that had resulted in the violent clashes in the Grosvenor Square anti-war demonstration."

Dr. Amit Kumar, an Associate Fellow at the Observer Research Foundation in New Delhi, is of the opinion that "Both India and Vietnam share disputed borders with China and both have learned the art of belligerence from China. With such competition for energy resources and regional power, the India-Vietnamese relationship would inevitably be driven by the need for hedge way against China."

According to Tony D., an expatriate from Southern California "When the American troops left Vietnam, the south had a corrupt and totally ineffective military. Two years later the north conducted a full scale invasion and overran the south. They began a reign of terror against anyone who had any connections, no matter how remote, with the former government. Executions and reeducation camps were commonplace. It was not until the mid 80's that these policies eased when the government paid more attention to the plight of the population. This also opened up commerce to international markets. This would not have been possible without the vision of giants like John Lennon and Yoko Ono. I am not, by any means, saying that Lennon and Ono did this alone. If one has a vision, anything is possible, and you must believe in yourself, no matter what others may say.

3

PAUL MCCARTNEY:
THE SECOND-IN-COMMAND

John Lennon is regarded as the founder of The Beatles. He deserves that credit, and his achievements as a prominent Rock 'n' Roll musician are noteworthy. A significant achievement of his – if one has to select one – is his recognizing the inherent qualities and potential of Paul McCartney and asking him to join him. Paul, in certain respects, has surpassed even his senior, John Lennon, by his "better songs", more congenial nature, and constant efforts to keep The Beatles united and keep Beatlemania alive. He is still active, very much visible, and has unlimited energy, even at the age of 70. He is like an EverReady battery, always energetic and enlightening. He had his differences with John Lennon, but never said an unkind word about him. In fact, it was John Lennon who envied Paul.

Paul McCartney was born in Liverpool, England, on June 18th, 1942. His mother was a nurse, and his father was a cotton salesman. Paul's childhood was much warmer than John Lennon's. Paul's love for the piano was in his genes; his father used to play piano and trumpet.

In 1953, at the age of 10, Paul won an essay competition about Queen Elizabeth's Coronation. Paul was very intelligent; he passed the eleven plus examination easily, and the best grammar school in Liverpool had no problem in admitting him.

John Lennon spotted Paul and liked him immediately. They were introduced by Pete Shotton, a close friend of John Lennon. Both John and Paul had lost their mothers early on in their lives. This was one more reason for creating a bond between them.

John Lennon founded a schoolboy band, Paul McCartney joined, and The Beatles were born. At the time, Liverpool teenagers were attracted to American Rock and Roll music artists like (The King) Elvis Presley. American Rock and Roll hit England big time, and John Lennon and Paul McCartney became early Elvis aficionados.

Buddy Holly, one of the premier pioneers of Rock and Roll, was also a great influence on John and Paul. Buddy wrote his own songs, and was an accomplished musician. This inspired The Beatles to write and perform their own songs, which they did together. The songs got better and better gradually.

John and Paul's contributions and role in The Beatles have already been described in an earlier chapter.

After about eight years together, McCartney and Lennon began to have disagreements, and this was also true for their wives. Paul and Linda's children were getting older. They were not spoiled, because they were treated like everybody else, and were progressing very well in their education. Bowing to Linda's wishes, the McCartney family resorted to being strictly vegetarian.

What Paul did when The Beatles were a group, has already been described. What Paul did after The Beatles' break up, shows his true stature. In 1970, Paul formed his own band and invited Denny Seiwell and Hugh McCracken to join. The Scottish atmosphere was not very congenial to them. The wives of the others were also in his new band. Paul very much wanted Linda to be in his band, but she did not possess the necessary skills, so Paul brought in an experienced musician, Denny Laine. The band's name was Wings. The first album they produced was *Wildlife*. The song *Dear Friend* in it was addressed to John, but it was a poor attempt, as compared to John's Imagine, which did the job of addressing their broken friendship in a much better way. A professional producer, Phil Spector, helped John to produce 'Imagine'. At this time, John was very critical of Paul and Phil was fueling the fire. The magazine *Melody Maker* was the forum where Lennon and McCartney were making critical comments about each other. Of course, money was the cause of this feud.

In 1972, Henry McCullough joined Wings, and Wings went to perform at Knottingham University. They played *Give Ireland Back to the Irish*. Then they went on their first European Tour. In Sweden, they were fined, as all members of the band were smoking marijuana. Paul was very miserly in paying the other members of the band and was acting snobbish. His songs were also not high standard. Paul wrote several love songs for Linda. Paul could not go to America at this time, because his drug convictions were the cause for the denial of his visa.

In 1974, he got his visa, and Paul called on John and had a cordial meeting with him. John and the other Beatles realized that Paul was right that financial matters had been mishandled by their business manager, Allen Klein. Paul, as a result, chose Neil Aspinall to head Apple

Corp. He managed it very well until 2007, and then he retired.

In 1974, on a BBC Television show, John blamed Paul for The Beatles' break-up. Actually, however, it was John who announced the break-up first. This angered Paul very much, and he stopped the production of the movie, *John, Paul, George and Ringo*.

Critics were commenting that Paul's songs were unnecessarily sentimental and meaningless. Paul replied to this criticism by his song, *Silly Love Songs*, which became a U.S. #1 for five weeks.

Paul met John on April 24 1976 again. This turned out to be their last meeting. Paul had a successful Wings Tour in America in 1976. The success was also due to the efforts of Linda, Denny Laine, Jimmy McCullough, and their road manager, John Hammel, who became his personal assistant later. McCartney Publishing Limited (MPL) was in full swing at this time. It had its headquarters at Soho Square in London. A triple album of the U.S. Tour, *Wings over America* reached #1 in the United States.

After the American Tour, Paul hosted a lunch in honor of Buddy Holly, the legend of Rock 'n' Roll, who had combined Rockabilly with Rhythm and Blues, bringing about a craze to the kids in the U.S.A. Ritchie Valens and Jiles Perry Richardson, Jr., (also known affectionately as 'the Big Bopper'), had died instantly killed in an aircraft crash. Paul owns the entire Buddy Holly catalog.

Paul's lyric, *Mull of Kintyre* is his best, after The Beatles' break-up. Two million copies of this were sold. It stayed at #1 for 9 weeks on the BBC show *Top of the Pops*. It had stayed on the charts, even longer than The Beatles' *She Loves You*.

In 1979, Paul's excellent solo new song, *Coming Up* hit number 1 in the U.S. He also performed some well-publicized concerts to help Cambodian refugees. Paul and his band sang, Got to Get You into My Life. The audience enjoyed it very much, because this was the first time Paul performed this song since 1966 (when The Beatles stopped touring.)

In March 1979, Eric Clapton married George Harrison's ex-wife Pattie Boyd. Paul and Ringo, but not John Lennon, graced this occasion, and performed Sgt. Pepper's Lonely Hearts Club Band.

A new album, Back to the Egg, came out at this time, and received a good response. Jimmy McCullough died and Wings had to recruit some new members. Wings performed at the Glasgow Apollo, where Paul surprised the audience by bringing in the Campbeltown Pipe Band and singing Mull of Kintyre.

Paul's Japanese Tour started on January 21st, 1980. However, it did not begin on an auspicious note. Paul was arrested because he was in possession of marijuana, and he was in jail for nine days. After that, Paul and his family were deported to England via Amsterdam: the Japanese did not want any undue publicity about this celebrity. The Japanese prison guards were happy to hear Paul play and sing Yesterday, after his release. From this time onward, Paul was busy with getting the band Wings together and putting out the albums Back to the Egg, Hot Hits and Kold Kutz and Tug of War.

When John Lennon was assassinated on December 8th, 1980, Paul McCartney got the news immediately, from his manager, and from Yoko Ono. Paul, by nature, is an unsuitable person for expressing emotions and reactions.

So, what he said, and did not mean, at this time, created some controversy among the news media. It was unfortunate that he appeared uncaring, saying only that the assassination of John Lennon was "a drag". In 1981, John and Yoko's album *Double Fantasy* went triple Platinum and was named Album of the Year. A Grammy Awards Presentation was held in Los Angeles. Paul McCartney, via satellite, saluted John for this album.

In 1981, Michael Jackson came to England, to meet Paul and get some advice. Paul jokingly told him to buy his songs. But Michael actually did it and Paul had to repent, as he could not lay his hands on them ever again. In 1982, Paul McCartney and Michael Jackson had a duet song, *Say Say Say* off the album *Pipes of Peace* and *The Girl Is Mine* from the album *Thriller*. Paul also collaborated with Stevie Wonder for the duet *Ebony And Ivory*, which became a hit in both the U.K. and in the U.S. The album *Tug Of War* achieved double success in both the U.S. and the U.K. On this album, Paul had written a song, *Here Today*, for his mate John Lennon. He faithfully sings this song in middle portion of every concert.

In 1982, Paul produced some movies, but they flopped. His close associate, Denny Laine, wrote articles entitled, "*The Real McCartney*" and this personal criticism hurt Paul, but Paul did not respond to it. Despite such setbacks, Paul McCartney was the richest entertainer in the world at that time.

In 1985, there was a Trans-Atlantic Concert known as LIVE AID, to aid famine victims in Africa. The concert was beamed by satellite to 152 countries. The viewers in the U.S. could see performances in London and Philadelphia. It was not just a pop concert, nor a TV show, but a means to keep people alive. Famous Rock'n'Roll musicians Elton John, Mick Jagger, Madonna and Paul McCartney performed at this concert. At the end of the programs, all the musicians came on-stage and sang, *We Are the World*. It was dedicated to the African Relief Effort and the audience also joined the musicians. $50 million were raised.

For a very large number of people, it was the very first time they heard a Beatle sing a Beatle number, Let It Be. This was pop music's great moment.

Through this concert, television was used as a tool and as a catalyst to draw the attention of the whole world to a humanitarian problem. Strands and phone lines were jammed for the Aid concert. A number of people and corporations donated their time, goods and services.

In 1985, Paul held live Aid concerts in Philadelphia, Boston and London. Prince Charles and Lady Diana attended the London performance at the famous Wembley Arena and were very much impressed with *Let It Be*. They invited Paul to take part in the 1986 Prince's Trust All-Star Rock Concert. George Harrison and Ringo Starr were also invited. Yoko Ono chose to decline.

In 1986, Paul had a setback. The Monkees, for the first time, outsold The Beatles, via their album That Was Then, This Is Now. This bruised Paul's ego and damaged his credibility. He, therefore, replaced his manager and appointed Richard Ogden. However, he and Paul had to spend a lot of time to please Linda in her passion for vegetarianism, and love for animals.

In the Christmas of 1987, Paul released his Greatest Hits album *All the Best*, of only Wings songs, that had hit Double Platinum.

The Beatles were officially inducted into the Rock'n'Roll Hall of Fame in 1988. Paul did not attend this function, explaining his absence by saying that he would have felt like a hypocrite, waving and smiling at a fake Beatles Reunion, even though The Beatles had unsettled differences.

In 1988/1989, Paul collaborated with Elvis Costello, who was a very talented singer and songwriter. McCartney's work discipline and his logical lyrics made a profound impression on Costello. Together, they produced the album *Flowers in the Dirt*. This album had many popular songs such as *My Brave Face, We Got Married, Rough Ride, Figure Of Eight, How Many People, Motor of Love, Put It There*, and *Ou Est Le Soleil*.

Paul embarked on a full-fledged Concert Tour, which he called *The Paul McCartney World Tour* in 1989/1990. He went from London to Oslo, Norway and then to the U.S. and Canada. McCartney thrilled his audiences, and people were reacting emotionally as they were especially nostalgic for his Beatles hits. His Wings songs, such as *Band On The Run, Jet, Live And Let Die, My Love* and *Coming Up* also drew huge crowds.

In 1989, Paul co-founded the Liverpool Institute for Performing Arts with Mark Featherstone-Witty. Paul donated 1 million pounds for this project to transform an old school into a state-of-the-art performing arts higher education institution. This project was very ambitious and required a lot more money, which had to be collected from The Queen, George Harrison, and Chevy Chase. The German electronics company Grundig donated 2 million pounds.

In February 1990, Paul McCartney was given the Lifetime Achievement Award, for his more than 25 years of sold-out concerts. This award was presented to him by Meryl Streep. Paul made a sizeable profit on this World Tour of his, which covered five continents. Then, Paul bid an emotional farewell to his band. A tour documentary, *Get Back* and highlights of his tour interviews called, *Put It There*" were released after the tour and were highly acclaimed.

Paul McCartney has been named by the Guinness Book of World Records as "The Most Successful Songwriter Ever." Paul McCartney has produced more number-one-songs than John Lennon has and even "The King" himself, Elvis Presley.

An Oratorio is a piece of music by soloists and choruses. It usually has a religious story as its basis. Paul entrusted the famous Grammy-Award-winning soloist Dame Kiri Te Kanawa with the task of creating Paul *McCartney's* Liverpool Oratorio, dealing with Paul's Liverpool childhood.

In 1992, Paul and Linda were making preparations for their (New World Tour), which started in 1993. He created the album *Off the Ground.* It was a selection of his Beatles' songs as well as Wings songs. These songs attracted a modern audience. Some prominent songs off this album and the tour are: *Off the Ground, Hope of Deliverance, Get Out of My Way, I Owe It All To You, Golden Earth Girl, Mistress and Maid, C'mon People, Peace In The Neighborhood, Another Day, Every Night, Let 'Em In, Maybe I'm Amazed, My Love, Drive My Car, Here, There and Everywhere, We Can Work It Out, Magical Mystery Tour, Penny Lane, 'Fixing a Hole, Band on the Run, Jet, Letting Go,* and *Live and Let Die.*

Paul was on the NBC hit show "*Saturday Night Live*", in 1993. Chris Farley, the comedy legend was pestering Paul with questions like, "Remember when you were in The Beatles?", and "Will The Beatles ever get back together again?" Paul did not lose his temper and remarked, "Chris, I think we all know the answer to this."

Neil Aspinall wanted to write a TV history of The Beatles. For that, he wanted it from The Beatles' own mouth. George Harrison was not really interested in this, but he was in monetary trouble, due to his spending habits. Also, his solo songs did much better than his Beatles songs. Reluctantly, he agreed to work with Paul and Ringo on this project.

Paul wanted to call it *The Long and Winding Road,* but it was Paul's song, so George objected to it, and they all agreed to call it as simply *The Beatles Anthology.* The three surviving Beatles wanted some way or another to bring John Lennon into this project. They approached Yoko Ono, who gave Paul a tape of John's unfinished song, *Free As a Bird.* The three surviving Beatles, now known as The Threatles, completed the song, with the help of Jeff Lynne. *The Beatles Anthology* was released on November 19th, 1995. It was an epic story on TV, which ran for 11 hours, in its expanded form. This project brought The Beatles' Apple Corp. a lot of money. Several million units were sold all over the World.

While The *Beatles Anthology* was being written, Paul's album *Flaming Pie* was released. It contained the songs: *The World Tonight, Little Willow* (for Princess Diana), *The Songs We Were Singing, Somedays, Young Boy, Calico Skies, Beautiful Night,* and *Flaming Pie.* This album went Platinum in 1998. Paul also had a hit album *Run Devil Run,* at this time. Many songs on this album were Ricky Nelson's hits. He was an idol of John Lennon and Paul McCartney, when they were teenagers in Liverpool.

Sir Paul arranged an exhibition of his paintings in Siegen, Germany, but this only exposed Paul's arrogance and vanity, as he was no good as a painter.

In December 1995, Linda (Paul's wife) was diagnosed with breast cancer. Paul gave up all his business and touring plans and devoted his entire life to look after Linda in her final days. In spite of her illness, Linda, with the help of Danny Fields and Neil Young, tried very hard to get Paul inducted into the Rock and Roll Hall of Fame as a solo artist, but she was not alive to see this dying wish of hers being fulfilled.

In 1998, Queen Elizabeth bestowed Knighthood on Paul McCartney. So, Paul now became Sir Paul and Linda became Lady McCartney. To celebrate this occasion, Linda presented a watch to Paul with the inscription "To Paul, my Knight in shining armor".

Paul and Linda attended the London Symphony Orchestra Concert held at the famous Royal Albert Hall, conducted by Laurence Foster. The music in this concert was very powerful and emotional. It revolved around the lives of Paul and Linda. Paul expressed his emotions about Linda by saying, "Whatever time that I have, will be with you forever more" Linda lived to see Paul receiving one more honor – the Fellowship of The Royal College of Music.

Apart from music, there are many incidents and stories and hoaxes about Paul McCartney. Producer Mark Ronson has been rumored to be saved from drowning by Sir Paul McCartney. Paul and Linda, many times, ran into Ronson's mother, Anne, on the beach on Long Island. That is when Paul supposedly did this noble deed. Paul does not remember this.

Linda McCartney finally died of cancer, on April 17, 1998. Paul was shattered when Linda died. The Threatles – Paul, George Harrison and Ringo Starr were together again for Linda's memorial service. George came, even though he himself was suffering from cancer. Yoko Ono was not present and was not invited for the second memorial service in New York.

The Taschen Publishers have published a book called, Linda McCartney – Life in Photography. Paul McCartney wrote a foreword for this book. In that foreword, he said that when he experienced her photography and experienced it personally, his feelings for her changed to admiration. She was a great photographer, and her subjects were always relaxed. Her love of nature, children and animals inspired her to find fascinating subjects all around her.

She had a laconic sense of humor, was intensely loyal, and was very protective of her family.

At the end of her life, when she knew that her end was near, the photographs she made were pure and simple. Hers was an example of a life well-lived as a woman and as an artist. Paul McCartney always made it a point to show her off on-stage, while on Tour. This was apparent, especially on his 1989/1990 World Tour and also on his 1993 New World Tour. Her photography is governed by the mantra 'A picture is worth a 1000 words.'

In August 1998, Paul released the album Wild Prairie, which consisted of songs written solely by Linda.

On December 14, 1999, Sir Paul performed with his Run Devil Run band for 300 selected guests. The same year, Sir Paul performed I Saw Her Standing There, and No Other Baby by Ricky Nelson. PETA (People for the Ethical Treatment of Animals) started a scheme of humanitarian awards in Linda's honor. The first recipient of this honor was the famous Playmate and Supermodel Pamela Anderson Lee.

Sir Paul McCartney's widowhood lasted barely 13 months. He met a model, Heather Mills, at a function where Sir Paul was to present an award in Linda's name to Juliet Gellatley. Heather Mills had lost her leg in an accident and was using a prosthetic leg. She was an activist in the Adopt-A-Minefield Campaign. She was becoming more and more visible, due to her activism and her story, about how she bravely faced life. She divorced her first husband in 1989, and called off her wedding to the film maker Chris Terrill, and became involved with Paul. She succeeded in energizing Paul and in helping him get over his grief over Linda's demise. But, she was not a music partner to Paul. Paul had to release this on his own; a CD which contained the melodies for My Love, Maybe I'm Amazed, and The Lovely Linda.

Sir Paul proposed to Heather Mills on a resort island off the British West Indies, and the wedding ceremony took place on June 11, 2001 in London. Ringo Starr and Sir Elton John were present for the ceremony. Yoko Ono was not invited. Paul's step-daughter Heather and son James did not attend.

Unfortunately, this marriage started off, from day one, on a rocky footing. Heather's selfish nature and temperament, dishonesty about her past, and habit of lying compulsively, became an irritant to Paul, and his musical career suffered. As far as she was concerned, her charity work was more important, and she was constantly grumbling that Paul was not supporting her. In many respects, she was like Yoko Ono and like what Yoko did to John, she became a hindrance to Paul's children, his friends and his band mates. She made the life of Geoff Baker (Paul's long-time publicist) miserable. She resented the fact that Paul was more famous than she was.

Paul never openly admitted their rift and defended his wife, but after only four years of marriage, he could not take it anymore, and had a bitterly fought out divorce. Heather was asking for an unreasonable amount of 251 million dollars out of Sir Paul's Estate of 800 million dollars. The High-Court was very critical of Heather and awarded her only 48.6 million dollars. Paul and Heather had a daughter named Beatrice.

This turmoil in Paul's life did not, however, prevent him from carrying on his musical career actively. His thirteenth solo studio album, Chaos and Creation in the Backyard was produced at this time. This album got rave reviews from critics. It received three Grammy nominations, and 1.3 million copies were sold. This album has two famous songs At The Mercy and Friends To Go. The latter was dedicated to George Harrison. Paul's creativity was still at its peak.

Paul's fourteenth studio album, Memory Almost Full, was released in 2007. Up to 2011, two million copies of this album were sold world-wide. The Record Industry Association of America certified this album as Gold. This album has two songs, See Your Sunshine, and Gratitude. The former is a love song for Heather, and Paul retained it, even after his separation. The latter is about his divorce.

Paul produced many singles also, such as Ever Present Past, Dance Tonight (released on McCartney's 65th birthday on June 15th, 2007), and Nod Your Head. Paul also has to his credit three albums Rushes (1998), Liverpool Sound Collage (2000), and Electric Argument (2005).

Paul started dating Nancy Shevell in 2007. She was the chairwoman for the Bus Operations committee in New York, of MTA (Metropolitan Transportation Authority). She has been described as the most glamorous trucking executive in the world. A reader aptly commented, "Does she need a ticket to ride?"

In Nancy, Sir Paul found what Linda gave him: someone who nurtured him, but who quietly cajoled him when need be. "Nancy is universally popular with all the people in Paul's life," said a source and further added, "This was not the case with his previous marriage: With Nancy, it is all very calm, happy and serene. Sir Paul's children, Heather 49, Mary 42, Stella 40, James 34, and Beatrice 7 (from Heather), all approved this marriage and were absolutely delighted.

The McCartneys knew Nancy for about 20 years. Their two families had socialized together in the Hamptons. Nancy was given the nickname, Jackie O, by the children, because of her style and sunglasses. Since Nancy came from a wealthy east coast family (she is heiress to an estimated $250 million fortune), everyone was comfortable that she was not after Paul's money. The engagement ring from Paul to Nancy was a Cartier diamond ring worth about $400,000.

Divorced or newly married, happy or sad, Paul McCartney always writes new songs. They come easily to him. He is the least spiritually-inclined Beatle, yet he agrees to give all of the credit of his success to God. He defines his Rock 'n' Roll religion with the simple message, "Be cool, and you'll be all right".

Paul McCartney has tremendous energy. It looks as if he is in perpetual motion. He has continued to collaborate with his former band mates. He had a concert in Puerto Rico in 2010, which was a part of his Up and Coming Tour. In 2011, he was busy with his On The Run Tour.

In July of 2011, Paul had the energy and showmanship to create fireworks on stage at Comerica Park in Detroit.

With his still strong deep voice, he kept the audience spellbound for three hours. He did a special favor for Detroit by singing Marvin Gaye's Hitch Hike and by visiting the Motown Museum.

Sir Paul made a film after his all-star concert for New York City in 2001. The film *The Love We Make* is a documentary about this concert. The film maker, Albert Maysles helped him in this endeavor. The debut show was presented in September, 2011. The Celebrities Sir Elton John, Jay Z, Mick Jagger, and Keith Richards also performed in this film. Maysles has included off-stage interesting moments also in this film.

In August 2011, the music magazine MOJO published an interview of Sir Paul McCartney. Its theme was *The Resurrection of McCartney*. The magazine contacted many famous people to find out why people still love Paul so much. Elvis Costello said that the level of Paul's music is such that it cannot be replicated, even in the Internet age. A prominent reason for Paul's success is that he continuously experiments and always sticks to his philosophy that, "Love is the way". Paul's music may seem effortless, but he works very hard, he has the ability to criticize his own work. He never just sits around, and always wants to do something.

Paul likes President Barack Obama, but not President George W. Bush. He was honored by President Obama, with The Gershwin Prize for Popular Song at the White House in 2010 and played *Michelle* in honor of First Lady Michelle Obama. His touring schedule has become shorter now.

In 2011, Paul McCartney recorded his newest album, *Kisses on the Bottom*. It has *The Glory Of Love* and *My Very Good Friend The Milkman*, which are ingenious classics from *Tin Pan Alley*, and are rich in melody. MOJO magazine describes this album as 'an elegant gem'. The song '*My Valentine*', which he performed with the help of Eagles star Joe Walsh, who had filled in this song with some nice classical guitar licks, on the 2012 Grammy Awards show, reflects Paul's state of contentment. The first line of this song – *What if it rained / we didn't care* comes from what Nancy said when they were vacationing in Morocco. His third marriage has definitely brightened his outlook. His is so enchanted with Nancy that he says, "She has all the things one wants in a mate". He also ended the show with a moving all-star medley (with both rock superstars Bruce Springsteen and Eric Clapton as well as with members of his current touring band, Rusty Anderson, Brian Ray, Paul "Wix" Wickens, and drumming ace Abe Laboriel, Jr.) from the Beatles' classic album, *Abbey Road*. Paul McCartney had auspiciously began the evening by winning an award for Best Historical Album for last year's re-issue of his mega-hit album *Band on the Run*.

Sir Paul McCartney performed the songs, *All My Loving, Magical Mystery Tour, Live and Let Die* and *Ob-La-Di, Ob-La-Da* at The Queen's Diamond Jubilee Concert to mark her 60 years on the throne. Paul has always been impressed by the Queen and has admired her for the way she handles her job. Who can forget the occasion, when The Beatles were awarded their M.B.E's at Buckingham Palace in 1965? McCartney fondly shares his remembrances of the Queen by commenting that, "It was a thrilling time. I grew up with the Queen, thinking she was a babe. She was beautiful and glamorous."

On July 14th, 2012, Sir Paul McCartney made a rare appearance at London's Hyde Park, during a concert by "the Boss" Bruce Springsteen, who sang both, *I Saw Her Standing There* and *Twist and Shout.*

Paul McCartney closed the Opening Ceremonies for the July 27th 2012 Summer Olympic Games in London, to rapturous applause, by performing *Hey Jude.*

Also in June 2012, Paul McCartney and the band for his *On the Run* tour were in Europe and had a three-hour concert at the Rotterdam Ahoy Arena. The audience requested him to sing *Ram On.* Paul obliged the 15,000 plus fans. Though originally ignored, the *Ram* album was later on much admired, due to its musical scope-from acoustic guitar to Orchestration.

Paul McCartney's new album 'NEW

On October 15th, 2013, Sir Paul McCartney released his Sixteenth studio album, "*NEW*". This latest album is a retrospective of his entire life. '*NEW* explores both the highs and lows of Paul McCartney's illustrious career, as depicted on '*Going to Work*' and '*Early Days*'. Sir Paul wanted to try new things, on "*NEW*", and he wanted to make sure that they fit in with modern ideas.

This album is produced by Mark Ronson, Paul Epworth, Giles Martin (son of Beatles' producer George Martin), and Ethan Johns (son of 'Wings' records producer Glyn Johns.)

At the ripe old age of 71, Sir Paul McCartney is well aware of his past, and even at this age, he still has everything to live for.

The last verse of '*Early Days*' is, "Now everyone seems to have formed their own opinion, who did this, who did that ..." Sir Paul states about that, "The fact is there's only a given body of people who really know inside out what goes on, in his career, and other people write about it; that's fine. But when they get it wrong, you just have to live with it."

On *New's* '*Early Days*' and '*On the Way to Work*' Paul reflects upon his pre-Beatles and Wings youth, and also about his past. He pointed out that with regard to fame, "Your biggest problem is that you grow out of your old skin, and you see people go crazy because there's nothing to anchor you anymore."

With the song, '*On My Way to Work*', Sir Paul describes his pre-Beatles job, where he worked for SPD – Speedy Prompt Deliveries. The driver of the SPD bus would let him sleep, and would wake him up when he reached the shop.

Also for this song, Paul describes his memories of Liverpool bus, including his childhood in Speke, in Western Avenue, which was a big dual carriageway and was the end of the bus route from Pier Head. Paul and his mates would dig through the bins on the bus, looking for cigarette packets. The cigarettes served as a symbol of life, where people came and went, and smoked cigarettes.

On '*Like Scared*', which is a hidden track on "*New*", Paul revealed that it is quite hard to say "I love you" to someone. He found the subject quite interesting. He stated that it's a lot easier to say in a drunken state like on, '*Here Today*' (off of his 1982 album "*Tug of War*"), which was a heartfelt tribute to John Lennon.

This 'New' album is certainly a treat for generations, and proves, without a doubt that Paul McCartney has well withstood the test of time, and is still a major force to be reckoned with in Contemporary Popular music.

Comparison Of John Lennon And Paul McCartney

Tony Palmer, a noted archivist, has written in The Observer that "If there is still any doubt, that Lennon and McCartney are the greatest songwriters, since Schubert, then we should surely see the last vestiges of cultural snobbery and bourgeois prejudice swept away in a deluge of joyful music making."

It is a temptation to compare John Lennon and Paul McCartney. Both are great Rock and Roll musicians. Both achieved world fame. Both have great qualities. Their work together as Beatles achieved phenomenal success and their solo albums, when The Beatles broke up, also were very successful.

John Lennon achieved Immortality, by being the founding Beatle and by his tragic, untimely death. Besides music, Lennon also achieved world attention by his activism about Peace, the War in Vietnam, and the legalization of marijuana. However, his career was marred by his inappropriate utterances, vulgarity, due to Yoko Ono's insistence and unnecessary envy of Paul McCartney.

In contrast, Paul McCartney's career is steady, his dedication to Rock music continued creativity, innovativeness, tendency to experiment, mature outlook, help and cooperation with friends and associates, the importance he has placed on family values, and infinite energy, lack of envy, and practical and pragmatic outlook, have endeared him to the world. In my opinion, therefore, Paul stands taller than John Lennon, though many others may not agree with this opinion of mine.

4

GEORGE HARRISON —
THE THIRD BEATLE

George Harrison was born in Liverpool, England on February 25, 1943. His father was a bus driver. George was never interested in school. He was obsessed with guitars and Elvis Presley. His father wanted him to become an electrician, but when he befriended Paul McCartney (because of his interest in Rock 'n' Roll), while riding the school bus, he dropped out of school and joined the band of Lennon and McCartney. He was only 14 at that time, but the band needed a guitar player, and George fulfilled this need.

George was different from the other Beatles, especially in the respect of attitude and personality. He was honest and transparent. He was generous and compassionate. He is described as the "wise old soul of Rock 'n' Roll music", though he was of the same stature as John and Paul, and was a founding member of The Beatles, he did not receive a fair treatment from John and Paul. They gave priority to their own songs on albums, and only a few of Harrison's songs were included. But, Harrison never complained, as long as he got his share of the money.

Fame never went into his head, and success made him uncomfortable. Often times, he became sarcastic and used sly humor. When The Beatles performed for England's Royal Family, and when their first LP, *Please Please Me,* ran for 29 weeks, George became introverted and depressed, rather than being elated.

George was a gifted Rock 'n' Roll musician. The critics respected his 12-string guitar work. He was very creative and innovative, especially when he was dealing with themes of loss and sadness, as is evident on the album *Beatles for Sale. I'm Happy Just To Dance With You, Roll Over Beethoven Devil In Her Heart, Think For Yourself,* and *If I Needed Someone* are some of Harrison's highlights. On the song, *Twist and Shout,* George Harrison takes liberties to enhance the texture of the song.

Tom Petty was George Harrison's band mate in The Travelling Wilburys. He says George had a way of getting right to the business of finding the right things to play. He never forgot about pitch and was always in tune when he played, and out came his signature voice.

All the four Beatles went to Rishikesh, India, in 1966, at the Ashram of the Maharishi Mahesh Yogi. George Harrison was more influenced by the Hindu religion, Hindu philosophy, Transcendental Meditation and Yoga. George appreciated and practiced the teachings of the Maharishi. Added to this, was also the benefits of his association with Pandit Ravi Shankar, the famous Sitar Maestro. George began to understand and also to appreciate Indian music. He started to use Indian Instruments along with Western strings. One can recognize this in The Beatles' Masterpiece *Sergeant Pepper's Lonely Hearts Club Band,* and also in *Within You, Without You.*

The word "Ohm" has a special significance in the Hindu religion. Because of Harrison's love of the Hindu philosophy, Harrison started using the Ohm symbol on all of his solo albums. His album *Living In The Material World*, and the album *Music Festival From India*, are evidence of his attraction to the Hindu religion and Indian music.

It is worthwhile to compare Harrison's contributions, when he was a Beatle to his solo creations, when The Beatles split. *Do You Want To Know A Secret?*, *Devil In Her Heart*, *Roll Over Beethoven*, *I'm Happy Just To Dance With You*, and *A Hard Day's Night*, are favorites of the musical critics. It has also been mentioned by fans for interviews for **The Beatles Anthology** that George Harrison's solo-guitar arrangements on *All My Loving* in 1964, and *Let It Be* have indeed withstood the test of time.

George is known for songs which have themes of loss and sadness. Good examples of these are *I Need You*, and *You Like Me Too Much*. George's best contributions to *Rubber Soul* are *Think For Yourself*, and *If I Needed Someone*. On tour, George would outdo Lennon and McCartney, with this song. George has used the sitar in the song, *Norwegian Wood*, and has used more Indian music in *Love You Too*. George has shown innovativeness, originality and charisma throughout his musical career. Good examples of these are the music on *Wonderwall*, and also on *All Things Must Pass*. These are his solo masterpieces. They both sold very well. The album *All Things Must Pass* was awarded the Top of Charts Honor in 1971.

The Inner Light is George Harrison's last song as a Beatle. *While My Guitar Gently Weeps* is Harrison's finest contribution on the Double Album *The Beatles (White Album)*. *The Ballad of John and Yoko* was also recorded during this period.

George Harrison's solo career spans the years 1968 to 2001. That means his solo career started even before The Beatles broke up.

In December 1974, Harrison performed at Madison Square Garden in New York, where he had earlier in 1971 presented charity shows for Bangladesh refugees. In fact, this was the first American tour by a former Beatle. Accompanying him were Billy Preston, Ravi Shankar, and many distinguished Indian musicians. His devotion to Indian musical and religious studies had made his music more homogeneous and smooth. It became more gentle, sober, and melodious.

The critics said that this event was not so successful, because Harrison's on-stage manner was curious, and because he underutilized Mr. Preston. Also, Ravi Shankar's Indian classical music went over the heads of the teenagers. Many thought that when he was a silent Beatles and was playing a smaller role than the charismatic John and Paul, he was more likeable. On the whole, the event was boring and eccentric.

His solo contributions include an impressive list of the following: Wonderwall Music, Electronic Sound (an experimental work using a synthesizer), All Things Must Pass, The Concert For Bangladesh, Living In The Material World, Dark Horse, Somewhere in England, Gone Troppo, Brainwashed, and Travelling Wilburys Volume 1 and 3. (There is no Volume 2). With the collaboration of Bob Dylan, Jeff Lynne, Roy Orbison, and Tom Petty this became very popular because of the song, Handle with Care on it. George Harrison's album Extra Texture (Read All About It) was criticized savagely, but he regained his reputation by the magnificent album Thirty Three & 1/3. His solo recordings, My Sweet Lord, Crackerbox Palace,

Beautiful Girl, True Love, Blow Away, Love Comes to Everyone, and Not Guilty have very pleasing music.

Cloud Nine became a major hit in 1988, because of the song *When We Was Fab* (a song written by Harrison to settle his differences with the other Beatles). *Got My Mind Set on You* was another hit on this album. In 1988, George Harrison and Ringo Starr were featured in the video for Tom Petty's hit song *I Won't Back Down* on the album *Full Moon Fever.*

Harrison toured Japan with Eric Clapton in 1991. The album made from this tour received high praise from critics.

George Harrison, with the help of Paul McCartney and Ringo Starr paid a tribute to John Lennon on the album *Somewhere in England.*

An excellent publication, **A Tribute to George Harrison** *(Gold Collector's Series, 2003)* describes George Harrison's albums and solo contributions in complete detail. Most of the material described above, in this section, is based on this magazine.

George Harrison became more comfortable after the breakup of The Beatles. Because of the influence of Hindu culture on him, he faced the situation philosophically, with maturity and detachment. His reaction was very well expressed in his song, *All Things Must Pass.* His songwriting ability reached a new high after the split. He got a good opportunity to expand his creativity in his broad-minded music. Some critics always believed that John Lennon was the only true Beatle, and nobody else counted. However, both John Lennon and Paul McCartney insisted openly that George made a hell of a lot more contributions than he was credited for.

Paul expressed his reaction to George's death, by saying that, "Knowing George, he has probably formed a new band in Heaven and is Rocking and Rolling with John Lennon."

Harrison married Patti Boyd in 1966, but she left him in 1975 to marry Eric Clapton, formerly of The Yardbirds and Cream. Then, George married his secretary, Olivia Arias Trinidad in 1978. Their son Dhani was born in 1981. The Harrisons lived at the Friar Park Estate, overlooking the Thames River. He tried to avoid publicity. There was an unsuccessful attempt on his life, by an unknown assailant. This did not deter him from writing more songs.

An Indian poet once said to George, "Blessed is he whose fame does not outshine his truth. Here we are in the Hall of Fame. The inductees are not chosen because of their fame, but because they express their truth through their music. George said that he tried to write songs that would still mean something years from now, and I think it's safe to say that in spite of his immense fame, his truth will never be outshined or forgotten."

Elton John remembers meeting with George Harrison in the 1980s. He vividly remembers staying up late at night with his fellow musicians, and George Harrison, who willingly performed the Beatles classic *Here Comes the Sun*, just as the sun was coming up.

George Harrison died peacefully on November 29, 2001, at the age of 58 in Los Angeles, where he was being treated for cancer and a brain tumor. He had a great inner strength of character, and was never afraid of death.

The world lost a great soul in the death of George. He inspired many and touched the hearts of many. The world lost an amazing player.

Paul McCartney was devastated and was very sad. He eulogized George by describing him as a great guy, full of love for humanity. Ringo Starr praised George for his sense of laughter and humor. Yoko Ono thought that George's life was magical. Bob Dylan called George as a giant and a great soul, full of wisdom, common sense and compassion. Ravi Shankar, the Sitar maestro was deeply affected by George's death. George was like a son to him. Together, they had many precious memories. Tom Petty, who was George's former band mate, from the Traveling Wilburys, admired George's superlative sense of rhythm.

The tenth anniversary of George Harrison's death was observed on November 29, 2011, by his fans and admirers, by arranging several concerts under the umbrella title: *Ten Year On - Liverpool Remembers George.* These events were arranged by Jeff Slate of the New York Rock Culture Examiner. He had great admiration for George.

George Harrison's unfulfilled dream of doing his own Anthology was later fulfilled successfully by his wife, Olivia. Martin Scorsese produced a two-part documentary entitled, *George Harrison: Living in the Material World.* The theme of the film is Harrison's spiritual quest. Scorsese wrote this documentary from the perspective of George, using George's own archives of thirty years. This documentary also has new interviews with McCartney, Starr, Yoko Ono, Martin, Petty, and Clapton. Harrison's other activities, such as motor racing, movie producing, and the restoration of his country estate, are also described in this documentary. According to Olivia, George wanted to do everything in life, and he did. *Rolling Stone* magazine has provided detailed information about this documentary in one of its issues.

The Influence of Hinduism on the life of former Beatle George Harrison

Harrison met many people, celebrities, royalty, and ministers in India, but, the person who had really impressed him was Pandit Ravi Shankar, the world-renowned Sitarist. He was his link into the Vedic World. George Harrison, according to Pandit Ravi Shankar, was always quite humble, child-like, and had a great amount of humility.

These are the endearing qualities, which the Hindu religion highly values, and which George Harrison was fortunate enough to possess. Throughout his life, numerous occasions had arisen where George Harrison was able to show these qualities in public. When The Beatles split apart, George Harrison managed to come around, once again, privately, with his close friends and confidantes, due to what he had learned from his study of the Hindu religion and its philosophy on life.

George Harrison, in particular, was transfixed by the teachings of the Beatles' guru when the group visited India, the Maharishi Mahesh Yogi. This was a turbulent time for the group. They were no longer touring. After the sudden death of their manager Brian Epstein, they were, for the first time, left without a director and manager. When asked during a televised interview, George Harrison told a reporter that the Maharishi had told them to "have positive thoughts, and that whatever thoughts they had of Brian, would travel to him, wherever he was."

When The Beatles had suspected that the Maharishi Mahesh Yogi had tried to rape Mia Farrow, a guest of John Lennon, George Harrison confronted him, and had immediately packed up and left for London. This incident shows the strength of George Harrison's enormous character, a gift, which he had acquired from the Hindu Religion.

Primarily, George Harrison had learned, from the Hindu Religion that "the vibrations, which were set up, by the soul, and the love and hate of each of the souls, with one another, are what cause the attraction of the souls, with another, from one life to the next."

George Harrison was profoundly influenced by Swami Yogananda's insightful book, *Autobiography Of A Yogi*. He was totally enchanted by it. Swami Vivekananda's book, **Raja Yoga**, was also instrumental in teaching Harrison about the Indian philosophy of life.

George Harrison felt he had a tremendous connection with India, especially in some previous life. He earnestly believed that "each soul is potentially divine", and that, "churches, temples, and the rituals, which we perform, are all to be seen only as secondary details."

George Harrison was truly blessed with the spirit of giving in the Hindu religion. He showed it by helping his close friend Pandit Ravi Shankar organize an enormously successful Concert For Bangladesh, in 1971, at Madison Square Garden for the struggling Refugees of Bangladesh. George Harrison once again created mass hysteria in the crowd with his on-stage versions of *My Sweet Lord,* and *While My Guitar Gently Weeps.* He was once more on top of his game. When his sense of religious fervor was high, he had set the primary goal of getting the word of Shri Krishna and God out to the masses.

George Harrison had a soft spot in his heart, for the downtrodden. This he had learned from the Hindu Religion. This was his gift to the world, in addition to his enormous musical legacy. He was able to achieve even greater heights of fame and allegiance from his fans after he had embraced Hinduism - so much so, that he even maintained relations with John Lennon, Paul McCartney, and Ringo Starr after their acrimonious break up over musical as well as personal differences in August of 1969.

When a drug addict and mental patient, Michael Abram, attacked George Harrison, in 1999, he saw the sanity in his eyes and had shouted "Hare Krishna, Hare Krishna!" Studying Hinduism had given George Harrison the almost God-like gift for showing compassion for others' suffering, even that of potential serial murderers, when most ordinary people would have reacted hysterically and had him immediately incarcerated.

George Harrison often pursued profound spiritual questions like "Who am I?" "Why are we all here?" "Where did we all originate from?" Where am I going?" He had felt, in his heart that such questions could only be answered, if one had a thorough grasp of the Hindu religion.

As a result, George Harrison's spiritual and religious identity slipped slightly. He decided to spend less time in the recording studio, and more time in his garden. The Hindu religion had transported George Harrison to a highly evolved spiritual place. Throughout his life though, his rigid beliefs in his Guru Bhakti Vedanta Swami provided him with the mettle as well as mental strength to withstand all of life's obstacles. Even in his songs, he was often able to reflect upon his Krishna consciousness and had often urged his fans, to adapt the simple mentality, that "If the Lord is in your hearts, and we are able to reflect upon him, and one another, then nothing else can affect us." Through changing the lyrics of many of his songs, in this way, he was able to attract legions of fans.

After his divorce from Pattie, George Harrison soon found solace, in the company of Olivia Arias, who was a secretary at Dark Horse. George and Olivia married in 1976. Olivia gave birth to a baby boy, whom they named Dhani, which means, "Wealthy Owner", in Sanskrit.

Out of respect for George's devotion to the Hindu Religion, his remains were cremated and members of the Hare Krishna Community performed the essential Hindu rites. His ashes were immersed into the three sacred rivers of India.

5

RINGO STARR –
THE RENOWNED DRUMMER

The junior most Beatle was Richard Starkey, later known as Ringo Starr, by the Liverpool public. He was born on July 7, 1940. He was plagued by health problems since birth. This came in the way of his schooling. Due to chronic pleurisy, he left the school in 1955. At the age of 17, Ringo became a drummer in the top British musical group Rory Storm and the Hurricanes.

When John Lennon, Paul McCartney and George Harrison went to Hamburg, Germany, Pete Best was their drummer. But, when The Beatles performed at the Liverpool Cavern club, their manager, Brian Epstein, came across Ringo Starr and was impressed by his effortless drum beat. So, he took the consent of The Beatles, fired Pete Best and brought in Ringo Starr, who now became the fourth Beatle.

In the beginning, Ringo was very uncomfortable because John Lennon and Paul McCartney gave him an inferiority complex. They used to blame Ringo whenever anything went wrong. Ringo tried to remain aloof and on good terms with them. However, Ringo was at ease with

George Harrison. Ringo achieved an equal status as a full-fledged Beatle, not by luck, but by merit. He became a star in his own right, and even John Lennon had to admit that later.

Ringo's first wife was Maureen Cox. She died in 1989. He met Barbara Bach on the set of the James Bond film *The Spy Who Loved Me.* She became his second wife. Credit is due to her for getting Ringo over his alcoholism.

Ringo has a song, *The Worst It Ever Was Was Wonderful.* Everything in it relates to Barbara. Ringo loves her and she loves him; not that they never quarreled, but underneath, it was always love. For him, she was always the most beautiful woman. They have a charity, The Lotus Foundation, which supports people affected by addiction, domestic violence, cerebral palsy, and cancer. Half the time they live in Los Angeles, and half the time in Surrey, England. He has a 17th Century mansion on 200 acres of Surrey countryside. This is a great improvement over the cold and damp house, where he lived in Liverpool. Some people from Liverpool were offended, when he said that he didn't miss anything about Liverpool. Ringo shrugged it off with the remark, "There are some people who don't want you to grow in any way."

Ringo was not lucky to join The Beatles, but The Beatles were lucky to get him. He is the only one of the Fab Four who does not get treated as a legend, but that is exactly what he wants. He is finally getting the credit he deserves. Rolling Stone magazine has chosen Ringo as the fifth greatest rock drummer of all time. Ringo's backbeat was unique. No one played like him. Ringo is always a thorough gentleman. That's why some people love Ringo, but can't stand John and like Paul.

John and Paul gave Ringo only a token song on the first side of every LP. Ringo did not get his fair share. *Act Naturally, Honey Don't* and *Matchbox*, made Ringo famous. John and Paul gave the hit songs *Boys*, and *I Wanna Be Your Man* as a gift to Ringo. Ringo never grumbled about being sidelined, as long as he received good monetary compensation. Ringo was a part of The Beatles on every tour, except once in 1964, when Ringo had to undergo surgery for tonsillitis, and Jimmy Nichols substituted for him. When Ringo came back, the other three Beatles greeted him warmly.

Ringo's first solo album was *Sentimental Journey* in 1971. It was on the Billboard Top 30. *Beaucoup of Blues* was another hit album in 1971. *Back Off Boogaloo* was a Number 1 hit in 1972. A self-titled album, RINGO, received praise from critics. A song called *The No No Song* on the album *Goodnight Vienna* hit Number 1 in Canada. It was about his experiences with alcoholism and drugs, when The Beatles separated in 1970. He was very depressed at that time.

In 1989, Ringo Starr released his hit album, *Starrstruck*. He formed a band called Ringo Starr and His All-Starr Band. He toured the U.S. and many other countries for more than two decades. Ringo was very considerate in giving a chance to each band member to perform a hit from their own career.

Ringo "only" made an estimated £ 200 million from The Beatles – far less than Sir Paul McCartney, one of the two main songwriters. As the only two members left to face old age, how do they get on? "We're as close as we want to be," Ringo says, "We're the only two remaining Beatles, although he likes to think he's the only one."

In March, 1989, Ringo was invited to the Bay Area Music Awards. Buck Owens (One of the legends of country music) and Ringo Starr sang a duet *Act Naturally*, which was already a hit for The Beatles on their album *Help!* It was also released as a single and it peaked at Number 27. It was also nominated for a Grammy Award.

Ringo may not have the best technique, he may not have played 'kickass' drum solos, but he still is the single most influential drummer of all time Rock 'n' Roll. He was the beat behind the most famous rock band of all time. Several artists, including Leon Russell, were inspired by Ringo Starr. Russell had covered *When Love Is Dying*, which was written by Brian Wilson of The Beach Boys. Leon Russell had also accompanied Ringo Starr at George Harrison's *Concert for Bangladesh* in 1971. He played his famous *It Don't Come Easy*, at that time.

Ringo's 70th birthday was celebrated in Montreal, Quebec on July 8, 2010. He and Paul McCartney sang the hit Beatles song *Birthday* in front of a packed house. Yoko Ono was also present and sang *Give Peace a Chance* with Ringo.

Ringo was in his early Beatle days, very funny and witty in responding to ill-informed questions by the media. He used to do so with a very poker face. He was responding instantly, snappily and impudently. Some of his witty replies are worth quoting: "Do you like being Beatles?" to which he replied, "Yes, or we would be Rolling Stones." "When are you going to retire?" His reply, "In about 10 minutes."

"Have you any brothers?"

"My brother was an only child."

"Did The Beatles come to America to get revenge for the Revolution?"

"No, we just came for the money."

"Don't you ever say anything but yup?"

"Nope."

"What would you be if you weren't a Beatle?"

"The Beatles' manager."

"Why are you wearing so many rings on your fingers?"

"Because they will not go through the nose."

"Are you a mod or a rocker?"

"No, actually I am a mocker."

Ringo has never pretended to be deep. He was the natural clown in the band, the friendly face that kids and grannies loved. He was the yin to the yang of John Lennon's caustic wit.

Ringo has written and recorded *Ringo 2012*, with the cooperation of his friends Joe Walsh, Dave Stewart and Van Dyke Parks. It contains a sweet song, *Wonderful*, dedicated to his wife, Barbara Bach. The song, *In Liverpool*, on this album is about his gigs at various clubs. He performed at the Ryman Auditorium in Tennessee, on July 7th, 2012. He is not planning to write his autobiography.

About Paul and his wife, Nancy, he says, "It is fun when the four of us hang out. They are caring and loving people." Ringo admits that George Harrison's wisdom has made his life easier.

Ringo and his thirteenth All-Starr Band opened their 2012 U.S. tour at the Fallsview Casino Resort in Niagara Falls, Canada, where he promoted his new album, *Ringo 2012*. The Fallsview Resort is the largest elegant resort in Canada, and is the Crown jewel in Niagara's wonders.

Ringo Starr celebrated his 72nd Birthday on July 7th, 2012 in Nashville, Tennessee, where he and his 2nd wife Barbara Bach and his entire All-Starr Band assembled to promote Peace and Love. Ringo Starr is very active even now. He continues to record new songs and tour in various countries and cities. In this respect, he demonstrates the same energy as Paul McCartney. In an Interview with Rolling Stone magazine Ringo says that everybody wants to be a star, and it is great to be loved by people. But, then he adds, "We wanted, first of all, to make good music, and we did".

Today the world's most famous drummer has a great life. He works when he wants to work and goes on holidays, when he feels like it.

6

PROMINENT PEOPLE ASSOCIATED WITH THE BEATLES

Behind any successful endeavor, there are always many sung and unsung heroes. Without describing these personalities and their contributions to The Beatles' Story, no book will be complete. In this chapter, we have selected a few such prominent individuals.

Brian Epstein – A Tragic Story

Brian Epstein did so much for The Beatles, but he has become a forgotten man since his death. Brian Epstein is remembered only for managing The Beatles, and for his mysterious death. People knew very little about him. There had never been a manager like him before: Soft-spoken, non-showbiz. Brian Epstein is the man who discovered The Beatles and was their super-efficient manager, from the beginning, until his death.

He was born on September 19, 1934 in Liverpool. His father owned a furniture store. He was expelled from Liverpool School at the age of 10, for inattention and for being below standard. He had a hatred for formal education, and was bad in mathematics and science. He became a furniture salesman in his father's store. At the age of 18, he was conscripted for military service. After ten months, he was discharged, as he was found emotionally and mentally unfit. Next to the furniture store was the North End Road Music Store (NEMS). His father bought it and expanded it. In 1954, Brian was put in charge of NEMS. He expanded from piano to wireless sets to gramophone records. He was also selling the music publication *Mersey Beat* and was contributing a column to it.

On a Saturday afternoon, Raymond Jones walked into the store and asked for a disc by The Beatles. The name Beatles meant nothing to him at that time. He decided to find out who The Beatles were on Monday. But then, two girls came into the store asking for a disc by The Beatles. On making inquiries, he realized that, in fact, The Beatles were a Liverpool group. Another girl told him that The Beatles were the greatest, and that they were playing at the Cavern Club. So, Brian visited this club, and observed The Beatles in action.

He found them to be captivating and having a certain magnetism. He heard their song *My Bonnie*. He found The Beatles to be charming, amusing and attractive. Something sparked between The Beatles and Brian, and a meeting was arranged on December 3, 1961. At that meeting, it was decided that Epstein would manage their band. The Beatles signed a five-year contract in Pete Best's house, on January 24, 1962. Many people were warning Brian that The Beatles were no good, but Brian had a premonition that the boys would explode, and end up bigger than Elvis Presley. The Beatles were Britain's answer to Presley or reply to Columbia's Cliff Richards.

Epstein made a good business decision by encouraging The Beatles to wear suits, rather than blue jeans and leather jackets. He told them not to smoke onstage and to synchronize their bow at the end of the performance. The clean cut appearance of The Beatles helped the band gain acceptance by the public.

All The Beatles, including John, were always happy to follow Epstein's shrewd advice. If Brian had not been there, no British or American TV show would have given The Beatles any time. Brian used the prestige of his record stores in Liverpool, to get recording contracts for The Beatles. Epstein had the firm conviction that The Beatles would be internationally famous one day.

The first thing that Brian had to do, after signing the contract, was to fire Pete Best, and replace him with Ringo Starr. The Beatles thought Pete to be too conventional. It was an unpleasant task, but he did it. In a short span of six months, Brian secured several record contracts for The Beatles, and proved himself to be a successful manager. Brian was devoted to his work, even when his personal life suffered.

Brian wrote an autobiography, *A Cellarful of Noise*, with the help of Derek Taylor (The Beatles' road manager and their publicist). Brian has said in his book that John, Paul, George and Ringo were the ultimate superlatives, and defied analysis. They never accepted any barriers, neither of class, nor of sex. He described them as magnificent human beings, utterly honest, often irritating, but splendid citizens. The book brings out Epstein's guardedness, frankness, self-confidence, and self-effacement. Epstein was a director of Northern Songs, the company that owned the Copyright to McCartney and Lennon's songs. He was also a major shareholder in

NEMS Enterprises, which itself was a big shareholder in Northern Songs.

In her book, *In My Life* Debbie Geller tells Brian Epstein's story based on the recollections and impressions of people who knew him, worked for him, loved him, and disliked him. It is a story of a complicated life, of a person who drank, gambled, and took drugs, but also had a superb wit, charm and ability to inspire loyalty. He caused a cultural revolution and destroyed himself in the process.

By 1964, The Beatles had become so over-exposed that everything of theirs – habits, clothes, views, was being discussed every day in the press. Brian is given credit for keeping a strict watch on The Beatles' contacts with the press, and a check on their bookings. The Beatles were marching ahead – Paris, America, Copenhagen, Amsterdam, Australia, and Hong Kong. Brian had to take care of the safety of The Beatles and their security, because everywhere they went the crowds were screaming hoarse in a frenzy of exultation.

The Beatles got a world-wide audience, because of his efforts. This stress of managing such a super group took its toll. As a result, he got into drink, pills and gay relationships. He made several suicide attempts, but finally, he succumbed to an accidental overdose of sedatives and died on August 27, 1967, at the age of 32.

Paul McCartney once said, "If anyone was the fifth Beatle, it was Brian." A non-documentary feature film, *The Fifth Beatle,* covers the last six years of his life.

He had only a little more than 7000 British pounds in the bank, when he died at the height of The Beatles' fame.

An offer was once made to Brian for selling The Beatles. The offer was for a 50% interest in all his management companies. Brian told this to The Beatles and even suggested that they may be better off with somebody else. The Beatles were speechless. Finally, Paul said, "Sell us and we will pack up completely. We will throw in the lot of tomorrows." Their loyalty to Brian was tremendous.

Brian returned to the financier and said, "Thank you for your offer, but I cannot accept it. I don't think all the money in the world would be enough." For Brian, The Beatles were not a deal, they were unique human beings. He cared for the artists in the way they deserved. He worked very hard for them.

Brian Epstein had a very honest and philosophical attitude for managing The Beatles. He says in his autobiography, "I remember primarily that I am their manager and not their keeper. Nor am I a parent with a duty to teach them manners, how to speak or hold their forks. I am not a school master to make them read or cultivate themselves. I am most certainly not their judge on morals or behavior. I am, simply, their guide and I am not myself absolutely certain how it has all happened."

When Brian was working in his father's record store, his policy was to procure a record if it was available anywhere in the world, whether it took six months or a year. He had a sixth sense for finding hit pop tunes.

Brian's parents were very proud that he made a success in his chosen endeavors. In the early days, he directed The Beatles about what to wear, how to present themselves, and also in helping them to choose music. John Lennon realized that Brian identified more with him than with the other Beatles. Brian acted as an emotional and psychological counselor to keep The Beatles together. He was a man of destiny who loved the role of being the power behind the scenes.

Bill Grundy once asked him, "What is the pleasure of management? What kick do you get out of it?" Brian told him, that the dependence of the artists and their loyalty was very gratifying. Also, the development of the artists gave him pleasure. Brian's pivotal role made him the world's most admired band manager.

Brian kept a boundary around The Beatles. Nobody could cross it without his permission. He controlled every aspect – public statements, deals, press conferences - of the professional careers of The Beatles. In public, The Beatles were at the front, but after the concerts, he would come to life. He was witty and intelligent, and then he would become the star of the party. Princess Margaret once said that The Beatles believe their M.B.E. (the honor, title, the Queen of England gave them) stands for Mr. Brian Epstein.

Brian was in Port Mieron, Wales when he received an S.O.S. call from Nat Weiss that everywhere (Birmingham, Alabama, Memphis, and in many bible states), they were burning Beatles records because of John Lennon's statement that "The Beatles were more popular than Jesus Christ". Concerned with the seriousness of this problem, he flew over; he was worried about anything happening to The Beatles. He was very protective of them. He arranged for a press conference for damage control. Brian advised John to own up to it and explain the remark.

On August 23rd, 1967, Brian had invited his friends to his house in Kingsley Hills, Sussex, but Brian suddenly decided to go to London. However, he had drinks earlier and his friends tried to dissuade him from going. He did not listen to them and went to London any way. Geoffrey Ellis and Peter Brown and a few more friends stayed in the house, even though their host had left.

The next morning, Peter Brown called Brian in London, but Brian decided to stay in London for one more night, as he was not feeling well. He wanted to relax. The next morning, on Sunday, Geoffrey Ellis telephoned Brian's London home. Brian's butler, Antonio, answered the telephone, and told him that Brian's bedroom door was locked and he was sleeping. After a while, Antonio called Brian's friends and told them that he was very much concerned about Brian.

Joanne Peterson drove to London and with Antonio, she knocked on Brian's door, but there was no reply. So, Joanne called Brian's doctor, Norman Kowan, but he was not there. Joanne called Peter Brown's doctor, John Gallway. She also called Allister Taylor, a friend of Brian. Antonio and the doctor broke the door down. The doctor's face turned white, and they all knew that Brian was dead. Peter and Geoffrey, upon learning this, immediately arrived. They were all totally shocked, and then they called the police.

The day after Brian's death was a bank holiday and an inquest was not possible. Brian's family was Jewish, and the custom was for Jews to bury dead bodies within 24 hours, but this was not possible for Brian.

Peter Brown and others informed The Beatles, who were in Bangore, Wales with the Maharishi Mahesh Yogi at that time. The Beatles were shocked and frightened – especially John Lennon. John thought that Brian's death would be the end of The Beatles.

The inquest was held on Tuesday, and the coroner gave his verdict of accidental death. After that, the burial followed. Many people felt that Brian committed suicide, but in fact, it was due to taking an overdose of Seconal in conjunction with alcohol. Brian was just 32 years old, when he died.

After Brian died, there was a meeting attended by Robert Stigwood, David Shaw, Vic Lewis, Clive, Peter Brown, and Geoffrey over who would manage The Beatles. Robert Stigwood made a pitch for the manager's post, but The Beatles decided to do it themselves. The Beatles were a ship without a rudder for a while. But, Paul McCartney arranged his Magical Mystery Tour and got The Beatles together. Peter Brown and Neil Aspinall formed a company called Apple Corps and Paul actively took part in it.

The Maharishi wanted to control The Beatles, but Paul and Ringo as well as many other friends like Marianne Faithfull, knew that the Maharishi was an idiotic, ludicrous little guy with no capacity for managing The Beatles.

Brian's death meant a good opportunity for many people to take over The Beatles, but Paul McCartney was of the firm opinion that nobody else had the flare, the tenacity, the wit and the intelligence that Brian had.

This is the Brian Epstein story. No wonder they called him the Fifth Beatle. Brian Epstein did so much for The Beatles, but he has become a forgotten man, since his death.

George Martin – Record Producer Extraordinaire

Popular music record producer George Martin was born in England on January 3rd, 1926. He was interested in music from the age of 6, although he formally had only eight lessons in piano.

He went to a number of London schools, but throughout his school days, his interest in music kept increasing. During the Second World War, he was in the Royal Navy as a pilot. After the war, he enrolled in the Guild Hall School of Music and Drama. He studied piano and oboe and the music of many renowned musicians, such as Ravel and Duckworth. His oboe teacher, Margaret Asher, was the mother of Jane Asher, who was Paul McCartney's first girlfriend. Sidney Harrison was George's mentor, who encouraged him to pursue a career in music.

After graduation, Martin had a job in EMI's Parlophone record label. At the age of 29, Martin became in charge of the label.

George Martin wrote an autobiography, *All You Need Is Ears*. The profession of record producing did not exist when Martin began his career. However, with hard work, he became a leader in that industry.

George Martin recognized The Beatles' talent and recorded them from the beginning. George Martin's autobiography provides an insight into the attitude, temperament and genius of The Beatles.

George had many successes in his record producing profession. He had achieved this, not just because of producing Beatles records, but also producing the records of several other music stars. Record producing was basically a job that involved decision-making about what should be recorded and how best to do it. At about the same time as The Beatles arrived on the scene, stereo recording came up. George Martin used this to creatively stamp his own signature on the recording industry. Stereo recording is much more complex. It involves stereo players, mono mikes, speakers, their placement, and a lot more. George Martin understood all these things, managed the balance between instruments on the tape, relationships of voice to rhythm, of drums to bass, and combination of all sounds, and therein lies his success.

Not only did George Martin not know of The Beatles, but he was also unaware of Liverpool. It was when Brian Epstein played a disc of The Beatles in George's office that he first heard the sound of The Beatles. When Brian brought The Beatles to Abbey Road Studios for a recording test, it was love at first sight. He was impressed by their personalities. For The Beatles, George Martin was a famous person because they were fans of Peter Sellers and George had recorded his debut album. He liked The Beatles' music, but wanted Pete Best out. The Beatles were also of the same opinion.

Very soon George Martin signed a contract with The Beatles. Martin wrote in his autobiography that had he turned down The Beatles, they would have broken up, and never would have been heard of again. On September 11th, 1962, George Martin recorded *Love Me Do* backed by *P.S. I Love You*. George got a taste of The Beatles' humor at this time. When he told The Beatles to listen to the recording and tell him if there was anything that they did not like, smart-ass George Harrison replied, "Well, for a start, I don't like your tie." George (Martin) did not find that amusing. The other Beatles told Harrison not to upset Martin again, as he was very touchy.

Though the first record, *Love Me Do* was not very successful, Martin was confident that he had found a very prominent group. His colleagues did not believe him and were laughing at him. Brian Epstein persuaded George Martin to go to an American publishing company. They contacted Dick James. Dick started a new company called Northern Songs. He owned 50%; The Beatles and Brian took the other 50%. Dick offered a share to Martin also, but he did not take that offer, as it would have been unethical, as he was working for EMI. He did not realize at that time, that he turned down millions of pounds.

This new company brought out *Please Please Me*. That was very, very successful and was followed by the recording, *From Me to You*, and *I Want To Hold Your Hand*. The Beatles, by this time, were full of enthusiasm. It was now like a new oil well, with oil gushing up and never drying out.

Martin's function in the early days consisted of organizing the artists, supervising the recording sessions and also looking after the artists and the engineering aspects. His specialty was the introductions and the endings. The Beatles learned quickly and eventually they became the masters. In the beginning, John and Paul collaborated and helped each other. Later, they wrote their songs separately. It became either a John Lennon song or a Paul McCartney song.

George Martin was not doing production only for The Beatles. Brian, Dick James, and George were producing other records too. For example, *Anyone who had a Heart* sung Cilla Black, became #1 to the credit of George Martin. Lennon and McCartney were good musicians with good musical brains. George had a very high opinion of Paul McCartney. He called him a good musical all-rounder, best bass-guitar player, a first-class drummer, brilliant guitarist and a competent piano player.

It is to George Martin's and Brian Epstein's credit that The Beatles' record sales in America were enormous, but it was only miniscule in comparison to what happened later. It gave George Martin a thrill and great satisfaction. They were all working frantically.

The Beatles never said to George, "What a great job you have done." George did not mind that, because he knew that The Beatles did not give a damn for anybody.

The Beatles amazed George with their ability to go on forever with good songs.

Martin writes in his biography that The Beatles were successful because Brian Epstein gave them complete dedication. He made them do everything in his way. Even so, The Beatles sometimes indulged in their own whims, as for example when John Lennon painted his Rolls Royce black all over. Brian had great respect and affection for George Martin. In June 1966, George Martin divorced his first wife and married Judy Lockhart-Smith. Brian threw him a party. There were eleven people there. Paul and Jane, John and Cyn, George and Patti, Ringo and Maureen, Judy and George and Brian. Brian gave all of them napkin-rings, which were solid silver.

The record company, E.M.I., was very mean about The Beatles' contract in the beginning. But, when their contract ran out, The Beatles took their revenge and E.M.I. had to pay through the nose. When The Beatles first signed with E.M.I., the royalty rate was 5%. Ultimately, the royalties became astronomical.

On August 20, 1967, George Martin and Judy were shocked to learn that Brian Epstein had died in his sleep. When they went to his house, there was a bouquet of flowers waiting to be sent to for the two of them, congratulating them on the birth of their first child.

George Martin continued his music production work, not only with The Beatles, but also with many others, over six decades. He produced numerous comedy and novelty records. His excellent work in music, film, television and live performances, was rewarded by the Queen, who honored him with Knighthood in 1966. He is one of the greatest record producers of all time with 30 number one hit singles in the UK and 23 in the USA.

Sid Bernstein - Revolutionary Music Promoter

Sid Bernstein was a promoter with an extraordinary vision and a great personality. He brought the British invasion, led by The Beatles to America. He was an agent, manager and promoter to a number of celebrities and stars. According to Arthur Aaron, author of It's Sid Bernstein Calling, Sid was "solid gold". Paul McCartney once told Sid's wife, "Mrs. Bernstein, your husband is one of the most decent men in our industry".

He was born in 1918. His father was a tailor. His childhood days were in the Bronx neighborhood of New York. He tried to become a promoter at the age of 14, by writing a one paragraph contract between a singer, Sol Strausser and himself, but he found that it was illegal as he was underage. He knew that college education was not his cup of tea and became entrepreneurial right after dropping out of school. He was successful in importing English bands – The Rolling Stones, Herman's Hermits, The Moody Blues and others to America. He helped the careers of James Brown, Ray Charles, John Denver, Joan Baez and Miles Davis.

But, the crowning glory of his achievements was to bring The Beatles to America for a performance at Shea Stadium, with the help of Beatles' manager, Brian Epstein. Brian was a sensitive businessman and their friendship remained until Brian's death.

Nothing succeeds like success, and Sid Bernstein continued to be a very energetic and active music promoter.

In his book he describes how the screaming girls in the audience at the first Beatles concerts wanted to shake hands with Sid, because he had shaken hands with The Beatles and the Fab Four were unavailable. The girls considered him the next best person.

Sid took a gamble by booking The Beatles for the concert at Shea Stadium. It succeeded beyond his wildest dreams and this event helped Rock 'n' Roll to draw big crowds, everywhere in America and elsewhere.

When Sid did not have enough money to have a follow up concert of the Beatles, he decided to accept checks for advanced bookings to be sent to his P.O. Box. To his surprise and beyond his wildest imagination, he found that only in a few days' time, the box was flooded with mail and the Post Office had to store his mail in huge sacks. Sid needed more than 15 assistants and relatives to sort the mail and acknowledge the checks. All such events, at that time, read like a wonderful story. The truth is, sometimes, more exciting than fiction.

In 1998, the City Council of Liverpool unanimously selected Sid Bernstein as the first-ever ambassador from the city of Liverpool.

Stuart Sutcliffe: Short-lived Member

Stuart Sutcliffe, known as "Stu", was an abstract, expressionist painter. He was a friend of both John Lennon and Paul McCartney. He was in Hamburg, along with them, on both their early trips there. He used to play bass. However, when he fell in love with the famous Beatle photographer, Astrid Kirschher, and when John and Paul started chiding him and making snide remarks about Astrid, he had a fight with them, and left The Beatles.

He was born on June 23rd, 1940. His father was a civil servant. When he was at the Liverpool Art College, he was known as a brilliant student. Lennon was introduced to Stu by a mutual friend, Bill Harry, who later became an editor of the famous music magazine, Mersey Beat. Lennon was very appreciative of Stu's marvelous art portfolio. Stu was a talented painter and was a legend in school.

Paul McCartney became jealous of Sutcliffe's relationship with Lennon, as he had to take a back seat to Sutcliffe. When Stu joined The Beatles, he started acting as their booking agent. Stu's friend Harry advised him to concentrate on art and not music. When Sutcliffe used to sing, *Love Me Tender*, he got more applause than the other Beatles. That created friction. Paul and John ridiculed Stu's size and playing. Eventually in 1961, he left The Beatles group and pursued painting.

As an artist, Sutcliffe is known for his British and European abstract art work. Sutcliffe's whole story and his decision to leave The Beatles are told in the movie *Backbeat*. Mathew Clough and Colin Follows have edited a book entitled, ***Stu Sutcliffe – A Retrospective***. Stu's passion for Art was not a hobby, but a way of life. In Hamburg, Stuart's fondness for Astrid intensified; he moved in with her, in her residence and continued his amazing art work. However, soon Stu started getting violent headaches.

On April 10, 1962, Stu was rushed to the hospital, but he passed away on the way. He died in the arms of Astrid. It was a tragic loss for her. Two days later, when The Beatles returned to Hamburg, John was very eager to see his good friend Stu, but the news of his death came as a deep shock to him and also to the other Beatles.

Stu's headaches and eventual brain hemorrhage was due to his falling down the stairs from Astrid's attic flat.

Astrid Kirschherr - The Photographer

Astrid Kirschherr, a young Hamburg based photographer, studied photography in Germany under Reinhart Wolf. She was a strikingly good looking young woman and belonged to a cult of a new form of modernism. In 1960, she met and befriended The Beatles, during their first visit to Hamburg. She became their close friend, and studied them photographically, and fell in love with Stuart Sutcliffe, The Beatles' Bass player at the time.

In Hamburg, The Beatles were starving for English food. Astrid and her mother satisfied their desires.

Klaus Voormann, also a friend of The Beatles in Germany, was a brilliant and talented young man with beautiful looks. One night, while walking around, he heard some wonderful music coming out of a deep cellar. When he went there, he saw The Beatles. His heart was full of joy. And the next day, Astrid went with him and she saw the wonderful figures of Paul, George and John. That was the first time Astrid heard Rock'n'Roll live. She found them absolutely amazing. However, it was Stu (Stuart Sutcliffe) who knocked her out by his looks and eyes.

The Beatles had their first photo session on the fairground location in Hamburg. Astrid's English was poor, and she had to use her hands and feet to explain to The Beatles what she wanted for photography.

Astrid met Brian Epstein in Liverpool. She found Brian to be a very sensitive, intelligent, great man. In 1962, Brian called Astrid to get some decent pictures of The Beatles in their suits.

Astrid was especially friendly with George Harrison. Whenever Astrid was in trouble with money, he helped her like a guardian angel. Astrid became for the public

The Beatles' photographer. Her favorite photograph of The Beatles is of George and John in Stu's attic.

Astrid has shot Beatles photographs in dressing rooms, hotel suites, train dining cars, while learning their lines, making small talk, resting or passing time. The Beatles trusted her completely.

The photos of John Lennon by Astrid show his knowledge and sadness about life.

Everybody loved Astrid, because she was funny, sweet, and had an attractive personality. But, she was also very direct.

Pete Best – The Beatle Who Got Sacked

Few people realize today that originally The Beatles consisted of not only Lennon, McCartney, Harrison, but also Stu Sutcliffe and Pete Best, who was fired, and replaced by Ringo Starr. Pete Best's story is a sad one.

Pete Best was born in India in 1941. His father was working in India, during the Second World War as an army physical training instructor. When the war ended, his family came back and settled in Liverpool. In his younger days, he became a part of the group called The Quarrymen, formed by John Lennon. Paul McCartney and George Harrison also were in the group. John was their leader.

In 1960, this group, (which later became The Beatles), was invited to play at the Kaiser Keller club in Hamburg, Germany. Pete Best was their drummer. He was the best looking of the bunch. In Hamburg, Stu Sutcliffe met Astrid, a beautiful photographer, and fell in love with her. John and Paul used to taunt Stu and make remarks and did harmless ribbing to Stu. When it went too far, Stu protested and one day Paul and Stu started fighting. Stu warned Paul and told him not to say anything about Astrid. Paul did not pay any heed to these warnings. When Stu had enough of these wise cracks of John and Paul, he decided that he no longer needed The Beatles and left the group. Never the less, his friendship with The Beatles continued even after the fight. When Brian Epstein became The Beatles' manager, he became especially friendly with Pete Best, because he was very good looking.

In June 1962, when The Beatles returned from their Hamburg triumph to Abbey Road Studios in London, a bombshell fell on Pete Best. Pete Best had no idea that he was being dropped by the other Beatles. A music group called Lee Curtis and the All Stars asked Pete to join them.

Pete thought it was some kind of a joke, and said, "Why would I want to quit The Beatles when everything is going so fine?" Even Brian Epstein, when asked, told Pete that there were no plans to replace him, and Pete started behaving in the usual way with The Beatles, drinking together and traveling together. But, after two weeks, when Pete went to Brian's office, Brian told him, "The boys want you out and Ringo in. They think that you are not as good a drummer, and George Martin also thinks so." Pete was stunned, and was thinking, "Why, why, why?"

It had been a conspiracy, but The Beatles didn't have the courage to tell him. They asked Brian to stab him in the back. Even Ringo, who was a great pal of Pete, was in on the conspiracy.

Pete gave this news to Neil Aspinall. He became very upset and disgusted. Pete went home, broke down, and wept. Officially, it was announced that Pete left the group by mutual agreement, but Pete knew that he had been booted out. This was done in a sneaky way. The firing of

Pete Best was one of the dark episodes in the history of The Beatles. Even John Lennon later admitted, "We were cowards when we did that."

The news of Pete's departure saddened many people. Many weeping girls called him at his door. There were lots of protesters. Later, when Brian Epstein met Pete, Pete told him, "None of The Beatles were man enough to tell me, and left the dirty work to you." This whole incident has been described by Pete Best in his biographical book, **The Pete Best Story.**

Pete never received any satisfactory explanation of why he was sacked, but some of the reasons that were vaguely explained were that he was too conventional to be a Beatle, not friendly with George and Paul, and that he refused to change his hairstyle. It's also possible that The Beatles thought that Pete would overshadow them eventually. On November 24, 1962, on the occasion of Pete's 21st birthday, when Pete was to perform at the Majestic Ballroom in Birkenhead, The Beatles sent him a telegram, "Congratulations, Many Happy Returns, All The Best – John, Paul, George, Ringo and Brian."

Pete formed a musical group called, The Pete Best All Stars, but as The Beatles were conquering The World, Pete was struggling with financial problems. At this stage, Pete tried to commit suicide, but it was unsuccessful.

Some fans asked Pete's mother, "Does Pete still have any regrets?" "It's like a cut," she told them, "It bleeds, it heals, but the scar is still there."

Eventually, Pete grew into being a happy, relaxed and pleasant guy. He retains very happy memories of his days as a Beatle, a certain amount of pride and undiminished affection for John Lennon.

APPENDIX I

Similarity between the message of Paul McCartney's
Live and Let Die and that of Bhagavad Gita
By Amit Kshirsagar

All saints say more or less the same things: nobody wants wars, conflicts or aggression, but still these are the things that go on everywhere. It is instructive to see two entirely different people advise the same thing. The famous Beatle Sir Paul McCartney, in his 1973 song, *Live and Let Die*, expresses a message similar to that found in the Bhagavad Gita, a 700-verse scripture on a variety of theological and philosophical issues that is part of the Hindu epic Mahabharata. This was a song he was commissioned to write for the James Bond movie of the same name. For reference I will use the Bhagavad-Gita, translated in English by Eknath Easwaran and introductions written by Diana Morrison.

Sir Paul sings, "When you were young and your heart was an open book, you used to say live and let live, but if this ever changing world in which we live makes you give in and cry, say live and let die."

In Chapter III, Adhyay VII, Shlokas 4-14, 25, 27 and Adhyay IX, Shlokas 4,6,8,10, and 16-19, you will find a similar message. Both tell us that we need to be spiritually non-attached to this materialistic world, pray to God to remove our woes, help our community and live and die in peace.

Sir Paul says, "When you got a job to do you got to do it well." The Bhagavad Gita says that you are to do your assigned tasks, without expecting any rewards or fruits. It is for God to do that. You are to do your part, in an unattached way. Any job must be done for its intrinsic values and not for some extrinsic reward, like money or fame. One should liberate oneself from selfishness and selfish activities. This attitude of mind will take you to a higher-level personally as well as socially. (Chapter 16, Verses 1-8).

"Happiness lies in giving to others and not by expecting rewards from others, even from God."

The similarities between even a Beatles the Bhagavad Gita show the universality of the Gita's messages. These same ideals are propagated by many saints, scriptures, and poets. Let us not let these good messages remain in books but rather come into practice.

APPENDIX II

My Interpretation of the 1993 hit Paul McCartney song "Off The Ground"

My main purpose of writing this article is to present my Interpretation of the hit 1993 Paul McCartney song "Off The Ground".

I will go through the entire song line by line, and will discuss, my interpretation of them. I will also make use of the Sigmund Freud book, "The Interpretation of dreams", which was a ground breaking Masterpiece in the field of Psychology, Philosophy and Thought.

I am a huge Beatles fan and have a large collection of Beatles Memorabilia. I have seen Paul McCartney live in concert three times, and everytime I hear the classic song "Off The Ground", it fills me with great joy, and gives me great comfort, in dealing with the everyday struggles of life, especially nowadays in today's Twenty First Century World, which is full of Terror and Uncertainty.

"There must have been a lot of heartache, for you to sink so low"

What this line is referring to is the fact that without understanding and love, nothing is possible. Too often in our daily lives we may feel that our way is the only way. This can only lead to breakdown in relationships, and social turmoil and unrest.

"There must have been a ton of pressure, Only answer if the answer's no"

Because too often we have a philosophy of life as it is "my way or the highway", we fail in our attempts to even consider viewing life from another person's point of view."

Too often we become so dogmatic in our views, that the result often is too difficult to discuss, needless to say life becomes so full of clashes, and strife, that everyday life can seem utterly unmanageable, and we can become completely upset, frustrated and bitter, for even the smallest of things.

"I need loving"

"You need loving too"

"Doesn't take alot to get off the ground"

So, in order to live a peaceful life, it is very important to understand each other.

We may not like, or even love one another.

This is a separate issue.

For example, if we cannot get along with certain people, then it is very important for our own self-esteem, and in order to reduce further clashes to agree to peacefully exist without them in our lives. Otherwise, our life will be in total shambles. It is my personal belief, that each person has a god-given right to love and to be loved by others. If this is not there, life is unliveable, in my view.

"Doesn't take alot to get 'off the ground'"
Throughout his life, and especially after the acrimonious break-up of the Beatles in 1970, Paul McCartney's life had taken a sudden turn for the worse, as he had a severe crisis of identity.

For the first time in his life, he was without a band, and was professionally speaking, completely on his own.

Financially too, Apple Corps. had gone bankrupt, and its new owner was Allen Klein, a friend of George Martin, and noted Record Industry Attorney.

Almost, for the last 40 years, Paul McCartney has written songs and played with everyone from Michael Jackson, Stevie Wonder, Elvis Costello, Carl Perkins, the Dixie Chicks, etc.

He is still trying to find popular artists to play with, even at the ripe old age of 67.

In the 1993 video for 'Off The Ground', Paul McCartney is seen to be flying around over the World, and especially over water, finally returning to his band and wife Linda.

According to Sigmund Freud's classic book, "The Interpretation of dreams", flying represents a search for one's true identity, and water represents eternal youth.

In the case of Paul McCartney, especially after the assassination of John Lennon on 1980, this has been true.

In 1997, after the death of his wife Linda to breast cancer, Paul McCartney again lost a crucial part of his life. Since his marriage to Heather Mills had ended in divorce, Sir Paul McCartney is currently struggling to keep his commitments as a father, to 4-year-old Beatrice, and his commitments as a traveling superstar singer songwriter. It is also important to remember that Paul McCartney had lost his mother, Mary, also to breast cancer, at the age of 15. So, his struggle for identity has been lifelong.

"There must have been a lot of magic when the World was born"

"Let me be the one you wish for, the one you call for, when you're all alone"

Although Sir Paul McCartney's life has been constantly full of magic, from his days at the Cavern club, Hamburg, Beatlemania and beyond, the one dream of Paul McCartney that has not quite come true is having a permanent lifelong lover.

"Though it takes a lot of power to make a big tree grow"

"It doesn't need a pot of knowledge, for a seed knows what a seed must know"

What Sir Paul McCartney is referring to by the word "power" is education, spiritual growth and self-confidence. The tree that he is referring to is his own life.

"It doesn't need a pot of knowledge for a seed knows what a seed must know"

What this means is that no amount of education and general knowledge can make a person successful in life unless he/she has the seed of self-confidence.

If a person is ingrained with the seed of self-confidence, from an early age, then anything is possible in their life.

Sir Paul McCartney's own life is an excellent example of this.

APPENDIX III

<u>**Tofu Wings – A Parody by Paul McCartney**</u>

On his appearance on *Late Night with Jimmy Fallon* which aired on NBC, on December 10th 2010). Sir Paul McCartney sang a parody of *Yesterday*, titled, *Scrambled Eggs*. The famously vegetarian McCartney did not want to sing a line about chicken wings, so he suggested tofu wings. This was a suitable negotiation which he and Fallon had worked into their back-and-forth, during the Final version of this song.

The words to "*Scrambled Eggs*" are as follows:

Scrambled Eggs
Oh my baby
How I love your legs!

Not as much as I love
Scrambled Eggs
Oh we should eat
some scrambled eggs

Waffle fries
Oh my darling
How I love your thighs!

Not as much as I
love waffle fries

Oh! Have you tried
your waffle fries?
They are
so damn good
that they should be
illegal

They are like
regular fries but
they are shaped
like a waffle

Tofu wings
Oh my baby
when I hear you
sing

All I think about is
tofu wings
Oh Did you bring\
the tofu wings?

There's a place I
know where I go
for kick-ass wings

We could
even get a side
of onion rings

Scrambled Eggs
Oh my baby
How I love your legs!

Not as much as I love
Scrambled Eggs
Oh let's go eat
some scrambled eggs

SELECTED REFERENCES

Andreas, Robert and Fraiman Richard (2010) *LIFE Remembering John Lennon.* Time Home Entertainment Inc.

Bartholomeo, Joey, Leonard, Elizabeth, Baker, K.C. and Cottier, Sharon (2011) *Paul McCartney & Nancy Shevell – He Loves Her Yeah! Yeah! Yeah!* pp.73-74.

Beres, Derek (2005) *GLOBAL BEAT FUSION: The History of the Future of Music.* Brooklyn: Outside the Box Publishing.

Best, Pete and Doncaster, Patrick (1985) *Beatle! The Pete Best Story.* London: Plexus Publishing Limited.

Browne, David and Wenner, Jann S. (2010) *RANDOM NOTES, The Lennons Come Together Rolling Stone* p.32. *R&R Lennon's 70th Birthday Marked by Reissues, Concerts, Movies* p.18.

Clark, Carolyn, Sarah-Jane, Eddie Fiegel and Adam Sworting (2005) *UNCUT – Collector's Edition 25 YEARS ON LENNON REMEMBERED.*

Clayson, Alan (2001) *Ringo Starr: Straight Man or Joker.* New York: Paragon House.

Clayson, Alan, Johnson, Robb and Jungr, Barb (2004) WOMAN THE INCREDIBLE LIFE OF YOKO ONO.

Clough, Mathew H. (ed.) and Fallows, Colin (ed.) (2010) Astrid Kirchherr a retrospective.

Cott, Jonathan and Leibovitz, Anne (photos) (2010) THE LOST LENNON TAPES, plus An Intimate Remembrance by Yoko Ono pp.84-88. THE LAST INTERVIEW pp.89-97.

DeCurtis, Anthony (2006) Paul is 64 And Getting Better All The Time, AARP The Magazine, pp.42-45.

Duffy, Thom (2010) THE LENNON LEGACY – A TRIBUTE TO THE CREATIVITY THAT TOUCHED GENERATIONS October 9, 2010.

Eubanks, Bob and Hansen, Mathew Scott (2004) IT'S IN THE BOOK, BOB! Bob Eubanks.

Fuchs, Thomas (2010) 50 Artists Pick Their Personal Top 10s, Rolling Stone Issue 1119, December 9, 2010.

Gear, Gillian G (2011) MACCA ATTACK, The Music Collector's Magazine Issue April 2011, pp.16-21.

Geller, Debbie and Wall, Anthony (ed.) IN MY LIFE: THE BRIAN EPSTEIN STORY

Graff, Gary (2000) Paul McCartney, Interview, Modern Maturity, p.40.

Hiatt, Brian (2012) Features: Paul McCartney: Yesterday and Today, Rolling Stone, Issue 1151, pp. 36-41, March 1, 2012.

Leng, Simon (2006) While My Guitar Gently Weeps: The Music of George Harrison. Hal Leonard Corporation.

McCartney, Paul (1993) Paul McCartney: THE NEW WORLD TOUR. MPL (McCartney Publishings Limited).

Moore, Ann S. (CEO) (2002) Love Me Do, Church bells,... People, Special DOUBLE ISSUE, pp.44-49.

Moore, Ann S. (CEO) (2003) BABY BOOM – Paul McCartney and Heather Mills, People, Rodgers, Jeffrey Pepper (2005) ACOUSTIC GUITAR: JOHN LENNON A SONGWRITER'S LEGACY, pp. 36-39, pp.40-46.

Scaggs, Austin (2011) Elton John: The Rolling Stone Interview. Rolling Stone, Issue 1124, February 17, 2011.

Shivadas, Vidya (2012) Harmony Celebrates Age, Volume 8 Issue 10, pp.42-47, by Vidya Shivadas, Curator for Delhi's Vadehra Art Gallery.

Suddath, Claire (2010) John Lennon: Thirty years later, he lives on. TIME, pp.73-74.

Wenner, Jann S. (2011) CHARTS From the Vault, Rolling Stone, March 15th, 1969 TOP 10 ALBUMS. IN THE NEWS – Yoko Ono's dance floor domination continues p.18.

Wenner, Jan. S. (2011) Night at the Museum, Rolling Stone, Issue 1131, p.36.

Williams, Paul (2010) Uncut, The Ultimate Music Guide: LENNON "You may say I'm a dreamer…" John Lennon 70th birthday collector's special October 9th, 2010.

Made in the USA
Charleston, SC
02 March 2014